Let's Talk Intuition

Ericka,

Embrace your intuition and be free! Be intuitive and blessed!

Darlene

Let's Talk Intuition

121 Questions & Answers to Help You Use More of Your Inner Guidance Every Day

Darlene Pitts

Published by
Intuition Connection

Let's Talk Intuition
121 Questions & Answers to Help You Use More
of Your Inner Guidance Every Day

Copyright © 2007, 2012 by Darlene Pitts

All rights reserved. No part of this publication may be used, reproduced, or transmitted in any form or by any means, graphic, electronic, or mechanical, including keying, photocopying, scanning, recording, and taping or by any information data input, storage, and retrieval system, without permission in writing from the publisher.

Author Photograph: Omia
Cover Design: Sallie Keys, Psynergy Wellness
Book Editing: Angela Reid, Color Me Purple Literary Services

Limit of Liability/Disclaimer: While the author has used life experiences and best efforts in preparing this book, she makes no representations with respect to professional services, such as legal and medical, and you should consult with a licensed professional whenever appropriate. The author shall not be liable for any loss of profit or other commercial or private damages, including but not limited to special, incidental, and consequential.

This book may be ordered through booksellers or
by contacting the publisher:

IC www.intuitionconnection.com

Library of Congress Control Number: 2010938637

ISBN: 978-097855893-2

First Edition, November 2007
Second Edition, May 2012
Printed in the U.S.A.

Contents

ACKNOWLEDGMENTS xi

INTRODUCTION 1

121 QUESTIONS AND ANSWERS 3

   1. What is intuition? 3
   2. What are intuitive senses? 5
   3. How do intuitive senses work together? 10
   4. How do I know if I have intuition? 12
   5. How do I know when I have intuitive experiences? 13
   6. Do I need to meditate to use my intuition? 16
   7. Can tools or rituals help me use my intuition? 18
   8. What are literal and symbolic messages? 19
   9. Why does intuition communicate using symbols? 21

   10. How do I interpret symbolic intuitive messages? 24
   11. Why should I use my intuition? 26
   12. How do I trust my intuition? 29
   13. How do I act on intuitive messages I receive? 31
   14. Is intuition always right? 33
   15. How do I know what my intuition tells me is real? 34
   16. Can I question my intuition about any life situation? 36
   17. How can I use my intuition every day? 38
   18. Why are some people more intuitive than others? 41
   19. Why do I have a few intuitive senses? 43

   20. Are some intuitive senses stronger than others? 45
   21. How does intuition transcend space and time? 46
   22. Do physical and intuitive senses work together? 48
   23. Can logic and intuition work in harmony? 49
   24. Are intuition and common sense the same? 51
   25. Why do I ignore my intuition? 52
   26. Why do I miss my intuitive messages? 54

27. In what strange ways does intuition answer me? 56
28. What happens when my intuition can't reach me? 59
29. How do my beliefs affect my intuition? 60

30. Can my intuition help me change limiting beliefs? 62
31. Does intuition work with the Law of Attraction? 63
32. Which feelings and sensations belong to me? 65
33. What does a pulsing feeling in my body mean? 68
34. Why does my mood change as I enter buildings? 69
35. What is a first impression? 71
36. What is the conscious and subconscious mind? 72
37. Can my intuition help me make the right decisions? 74
38. When will intuition guide me to change directions? 77
39. When will my intuition pass on new guidance? 78

40. Is it normal to receive intuitive messages as I wake up at different times? 80
41. Can my intuition help me find inner peace? 81
42. Why do I feel an urge to call or visit someone? 82
43. Why do I think about someone I last saw years ago? 84
44. Why do things boost or drain my energy? 86
45. How can I know to be in the right place at the right time when opportunities knock? 89
46. Can my intuition help me with my business? 90
47. How can I sense when people lie to me? 92
48. Can people use their intuition to manipulate me? 93
49. How do I sense people as they are and not as they seem? 95

50. How do I sense situations as they are and not as they seem? . 97
51. How do I sense constructive criticism? 98
52. Can my intuition reveal my hidden strengths? 99
53. Why do I doubt my intuition in bad relationships 101
54. How can I sense if my spouse is cheating on me? 103

Contents ❖ vii

55. How do I use my intuition to find a good personal relationship?...104
56. Can my intuition help solve relationship problems? 106
57. Why do I intuitively hear music?...107
58. How can I intuitively hear low intuitive sounds?....................110
59. How can I hear my phone ring before it rings?......................111

60. Can I use my intuition while I'm in poor health?...................111
61. How do I speak truthful things while I'm angry?...................113
62. Can I use my intuition while I'm stressed?..............................114
63. Can my intuition help me reduce stress? 115
64. Does intuition outperform emotional intelligence? 118
65. How does my intuition cue me to reinvent myself?...............120
66. How can I use my intuition to be more creative? 121
67. How does my intuition put things in perspective?.................123
68. Can I intuitively study for school?..124
69. How do I sense when my computer will fail?.........................126

70. How do I use my intuition to protect my finances?..............127
71. How do I discover what I love to do?......................................129
72. How does my intuition improve time management?............131
73. Can I use my intuition to avoid vehicle accidents? 134
74. Why is intuition unpredictable? 137
75. Is it my intuition talking to me while I hesitate?....................138
76. Can I change what my intuition says will happen? 140
77. What is psychological anxiety vs. intuitive anxiety? 141
78. Does my intuition guide me when I exercise? 143
79. How does my intuition reveal people's motives? 145

80. Can I sense why a friend stops talking to me?........................147
81. How can I use my intuition to change people?......................148
82. How does intuition inform me when to let go?....................150
83. Can my intuition tell me if a situation will end well?.............152
84. What are precognition and retrocognition?............................154
85. Why do I sense things when people come near me? 155

86. Can my intuition help me find lost objects? 157
87. Can my intuition help me find missing loved ones? 159
88. How do I sense where to relocate? 161
89. Can my intuition guide my words? 162

90. How do I use intuition at work? 163
91. Does my intuition guide me on foods to eat? 165
92. Can I sense health problems? 167
93. Can my intuition warn me about danger? 169
94. How does intuition alert me to important signs? 171
95. How does déjà vu relate to intuition? 174
96. How do the chakras relate to intuition? 175
97. Can people more than fifty years old learn to use their intuition? 177
98. Are people born with a veil more intuitive? 178
99. Are women more intuitive than men? 179

100. Are children more intuitive than adults? 181
101. How do I help my children use their intuition? 183
102. Can I discern other people's intuitive messages? 184
103. How do I sense when to give others messages? 185
104. What is psychometry? 188
105. What is intuitive touch? 190
106. What is scrying? 192
107. What is a medical intuitive? 193
108. What is an intuitive investigator? 195
109. How do I handle truth shocks from my intuition? 197

110. Why do I feel a high while using my intuition? 200
111. Why do I feel lonely as my intuition advances? 201
112. How do I use my intuition to sense auras? 202
113. What is the difference between ghosts and spirits? 205
114. How do I know which inner voice is my own? 207

115. How can I slow my thoughts to notice my intuitive messages? 210
116. How are energy imprints sensed? 211
117. Do angels communicate to me via my intuition? 213
118. How does intuition work with the white light? 216
119. How do people sense when others will pass away? 217

120. How can I sense when loved ones are around me? 220
121. How can I improve my intuition? 221

AFTERWORD **227**
ABOUT THE AUTHOR **229**
INDEX **231**

Acknowledgments

I thank God for my gift of intuition and its infinite power. Thanks to everyone who asks questions about intuition for spiritual growth and an intuitive way of living. My deepest appreciation goes to family, friends, clients, associates, and others who share their intuitive experiences with me in public and private locations. By sharing, we teach to and learn from each other. I am blessed to be a part of each person's spiritual/human journey.

The Stairs

Leaving is beginning.
Step by step you arrive
At destinations you long to go, must go
Inside and outside yourself.

Your journey calls you to many faces and places that
Inspire you and tire you and rewire you
To live your brilliance.
What choices do you make with intuition guiding you?
What choices make you?

Look back only to remember how far you've come
With or without others cheering you on.
Look onward as your intuition climbs
Higher than free butterflies.

—Darlene Pitts

Introduction

Your intuition is a magnificent spiritual gift from God. This inner guidance allows you to sense the truth in life—past, present, and future. Truth is indestructible and reigns free of four human traps: disguises, delusions, divisions, and deceptions. When you trust and act on your intuition, you also reign free of human traps.

You are an eternal spiritual being, clothed in a temporary human body, undertaking a divine earthly mission. Whatever your mission, using more of your inner guidance every day helps you maintain an intuitive perspective of reality, size up people and situations, stay safe and well, and accomplish your dreams.

My first book *Discover Your Intuition* describes how your intuition uses eight intuitive senses to communicate intuitive messages to you. This book *Let's Talk Intuition* provides comprehensive answers for 121 questions clients have asked me about their intuition and intuition in general. Perhaps you have asked similar questions to obtain explanations for your intuitive experiences, which are a natural part of life and increasing in frequency.

This book includes realistic examples and true intuitive experiences to show you what happens each year, as your intuition communicates thousands of intuitive messages ranging from ordinary to extraordinary and beyond. True intuitive experiences leave out people's names to protect their privacy. Inner power points ❋ summarize answers for living the intuitive way—a life devoted to intuitive knowledge, trust, and action.

Start with the first fifteen questions and answers to build an enduring foundation for understanding how and why your intuition communicates intuitive messages to you each day. Read the remaining questions and answers in any order.

You're born into this world to function using more than your intelligence, willpower, and common sense. These will drive you only so far up to the peaks and so far down into the depths marking your spiritual/human journey. Your intuition empowers you to meet life head on and fulfill your life purpose wherever you are and whatever your circumstances.

Let's Talk Intuition!

121 Questions and Answers

1. What is intuition?

Intuition is your natural ability to sense the truth about people, places, things, and situations without using logic, physical senses, or prior knowledge. These factors support your intuition but have human limitations. Logic is a method of reasoning viewed as valid or faulty. It seeks facts prone to mistakes and manipulations. Physical senses include sight, touch, hearing, smell, and taste. However, these can be deceived by cunning appearances and actions. Prior knowledge comes from people, technology, and publications, which are sometimes inaccurate or outdated.

Recall the times you said, "I wish I'd known 'that' would happen." "That" could have been a surprise birthday party, home repair expense, or shopping mall rampage. Now recall how beforehand you sensed "something" interrupted your breathing or "something" prepared to explode. And you ignored your inner guidance because it seemed illogical, pointless, or passé. Yet, what you sensed happened like a movie rerun after your intuition forewarned you.

Recall the times you asked, "How did I know those details?" The details could have been exam answers, job offers, or natural disasters. Now recall how you sensed information that seemed impossible to know without observing it, hearing it, or reading it. Your intuition knew and downloaded the details into your awareness.

Intuitive awareness awakens your inner power. You realize when you sense the truth about someone or something. The truth is indisputable whether you accept or reject it. Your intuition keeps you informed—in the intuitive loop—to help you make knowledgeable choices with optimal outcomes.

Using more of your inner guidance every day helps you live from the inside out, not from the outside in. You sense what other people will say and do, which locations to visit or bypass, how objects are safe or harmful, when situations will go well or invite chaos—and so on. Essentially, you sense life and its players and performances with intuitive precision while you're awake and asleep. Your intuition supports your best interests and answers your heartfelt questions, including those you never know to ask.

Intuitive Messages

Intuitive messages are insightful communication revealing the quintessence of things with variants: who, what, when, where, how, and why. These variants relate to different areas of life, such as career, finances, health, relationships, and travel. Imagine that intuitive messages are like letters, emails, text messages, media transmissions, or phone calls. Instead of courier services and electronic devices delivering them to you, your intuition sends them free of charge.

You sense quiet or loud intuitive messages: Watch where you sit. Watch it! Be careful what you say. Remain silent! Run for cover. Hide yourself now! Loud intuitive messages happen before and during significant and life-threatening situations when you're close to missing or ignoring quiet intuitive messages.

Intuitive Journal

Create an intuitive journal to record, track, and validate your intuitive experiences. These are your direct spiritual encounters with things seen and unseen—often unexplainable by scientific measures. Your journal can be a notebook, diary, scrapbook, or computer file.

Weekly or monthly analyze your intuitive experiences for patterns and frequency. You'll discover the regularity at which your intuition communicates intuitive messages to you. You'll also discover your intuitive style: the various ways your intuition communicates to you.

> Your intuition guides and protects you
> twenty-four hours every day.

2. What are intuitive senses?

Intuitive senses are the eight sensing methods your intuition uses to communicate—independently or jointly—intuitive messages to you. Your physical senses (sight, touch, hearing, taste, and smell) function from outside in and inside out and on a corporal level. Your intuitive senses (seeing, feeling, hearing, knowing, tasting, smelling, speaking, and singing) function from inside out and on a spiritual level.

INTUITIVE SEEING

Intuitive seeing is the ability to see revealing images in inner and outer visions and dreams. Your physical eyes are open or closed as this happens. Visions and dreams contain images that flash like a camera snapshot, pause like a freeze frame, or roll like a motion picture "out in space" or in your mind's eye located within your forehead. Images include people, objects, and words.

Examples: Intuitive Images

Vincent drives on a highway. He intuitively sees a flashing inner vision show a secondary road at which to turn right to reach his destination. The vision warns him of a highway accident blocking traffic straight ahead. He's too far away for his physical eyes to see it.

Kim works on a lofty creative project. She intuitively sees a rolling outer vision show an ingenious technique to complete the project. It leads to trendy artwork.

Hernando intuitively dreams he builds a beautiful crystal building on commercial property. He wakes up and discerns that his career goals need to crystallize for him to achieve corporate success.

INTUITIVE FEELING

Intuitive feeling is the ability to perceive information via diverse feelings or sensations within your body. This happens with or without you touching external stimuli—a physical agent provoking an interest or a reaction. Feelings include hunches, impulses, and urges. Sensations include chills, goose bumps, and stomach knots.

Examples: Intuitive Feelings and Sensations

Sheila meets a group of business executives for the first time. In her solar plexus, she intuitively feels pleasant vibes (effective leaders) and unpleasant vibes (ineffective leaders) while shaking their hands.

Melvin shops in an outlet mall and is exhausted by the time he arrives back to his truck. His energy drain indicates that he intuitively feels and absorbs positive and negative energies of store employees and customers.

A neighbor asks Bridgette for her opinion about a family matter. In her chest, she intuitively feels a resistant feeling that indicates to remain silent to avoid getting wedged in a blame game.

INTUITIVE HEARING

Intuitive hearing is the ability to hear various sounds "out in space" or in your head (temporal lobes), throat (inner ear), or heart. You intuitively hear the sounds even if your physical ears are clear, blocked, or aching. Sounds include music, voices, and noises.

Examples: Intuitive Sounds

Chauncey intuitively hears a fast country song play in his head. He switches on the radio and physically hears the same song.

Angela sits next to a stranger in an airport terminal. In her throat, she intuitively hears his thoughts. She repeats them as though they're her thoughts. He gasps, "I was thinking the same thing!"

"Out in space," Phillip intuitively hears his cell phone ring seconds before it electronically rings. Then he intuitively hears the numerical name of the unexpected caller.

INTUITIVE KNOWING

Intuitive knowing is the ability to know information without knowing how and without a doubt. Information pops into the crown of your head "out of the blue."

Examples: Intuitive Knowings

Marcia intuitively knows when to exit a room or leave an outdoor space before adverse events occur there.

Brandon intuitively knows which local basketball teams will win playoff games despite their regular season records.

Tamika intuitively knows where to find missing people displayed on posted flyers, though she's never met them.

INTUITIVE TASTING

Intuitive tasting is the ability to taste various substances without putting anything in your mouth. Edible tastes include fruits, vegetables, and beverages. Inedible tastes include clothing, concrete, and lumber. Distinct tastes include music, emotions, and motives.

Examples: Intuitive Tastes

Jon hears state politicians speak at a local fundraiser. Their campaign promises intuitively taste mild (honest) or spicy (dishonest) to him.

Frieda intuitively tastes paper money signifying a financial windfall. A distant uncle passes away and leaves her an inheritance.

Manuel intuitively tastes sharp pain on his tongue two hours earlier than his daughter's afternoon soccer game. In the third quarter, she falls face down and bites her tongue.

INTUITIVE SMELLING

Intuitive smelling is the ability to smell various scents "out in space" or in your inner nose. You intuitively smell these scents even if your physical nose is open, congested, or bleeding. Regular scents include perfumes, flowers, and foods. Distinct scents include numbers, colors, and diseases.

Examples: Intuitive Scents

Strolling into a movie theater, Cindy intuitively smells buttery surprises signifying free tickets for the first four patrons.

Roberto searches for his wallet and intuitively smells shampoo. He finds it lying on the bathroom sink near a bottle of shampoo.

Riding her bicycle, Brandy intuitively smells hot chicken soup. The scent signals her deceased grandmother's spiritual visit. Her grandmother loved making chicken soup for sick relatives.

INTUITIVE SPEAKING

Intuitive speaking is the ability to speak abrupt, insightful sayings to others and yourself without thinking what to say. You outwardly or inwardly speak the sayings using your inner voice.

Examples: Intuitive Sayings

Ralph intuitively speaks the precise wisdom a co-worker starts to say about union leaders' job responsibilities.

Arlene intuitively speaks an off-the-cuff solution that unravels her cousin's legal problem.

Dennis intuitively speaks spontaneous words that encourage high school juniors contemplating future careers.

INTUITIVE SINGING

Intuitive singing is the ability to sing sudden, edifying songs to others and yourself without hearing external music. You outwardly or inwardly sing the songs using your inner voice.

Examples: Intuitive Songs

Jackson intuitively sings Leo Sayer's song "You Make Me Feel Like Dancing." The song energizes him on Monday mornings.

Harley intuitively sings, "Get well by Saturday. Call me on Sunday." The impromptu chorus comforts an injured friend.

Anthony intuitively sings the *Sesame Street* theme song to quiet his hyperactive six-year-old nephew. His intuitive strategy works.

SPIRITUAL BODY AND PHYSICAL BODY

Your intuitive senses belong to your spiritual body. They function in or near the same areas as your physical senses, which belong to your physical body. This functioning happens by divine design. Otherwise, you might feel awkward if your mind's eye exists on your shoulder while your physical eyes are on your face. Or your inner voice speaks through your knees while your physical voice speaks through your mouth. Your boundless intuitive senses transcend space and time, unlike your limited physical senses (see Question 21).

INTUITIVE EXPRESSIONS

Intuitive expressions are the diverse ways your intuitive senses communicate intuitive messages to you. Each intuitive sense uses its own communication methods: intuitive seeing (images), intuitive feeling (feelings and sensations), intuitive hearing (sounds), intuitive knowing (knowings), intuitive tasting (tastes), intuitive smelling (scents), intuitive speaking (sayings), and intuitive singing (songs).

During or after your intuitive experiences, identify which intuitive sense communicates or communicated to you and its direct intuitive expression. Notice if you've said or heard someone say the following intuitive expressions:

"A flash of insight hit me."
"I had a gut feeling."
"Something told me."
"I just knew it."
"Their words tasted funny."
"I smelled trouble in the air."
"I talked it up."
"A song came out of nowhere."

Intuitive knowledge arrives and unawareness departs.
Listen to your inward and outward intuitive expressions
and carry out appropriate actions.

---

3. How do intuitive senses work together?

Intuitive senses work independently or jointly. The latter uses five collaborating intuitive strategies:

1) Joint Intuitive Communication: Two or more intuitive senses jointly communicate intuitive messages. Rajah intuitively feels soft feelings in her heart. In her temporal lobes, she intuitively hears two babies cry. Rajah senses the early births of her sister's twin sons.

2) Simultaneous Intuitive Communication: The eight intuitive senses simultaneously communicate intuitive messages. Sashay intuitively sees a rolling outer vision show a sleeping rock dove. Intuitively feels calmness in her spirit. Intuitively hears a mellow song play in her inner ear. Intuitively knows tranquillity greets her. Intuitively tastes smooth ice cream. Intuitively smells perpetual serenity. Intuitively speaks a graceful meditation. Intuitively sings "Peace Be Still." Sasha senses a peaceful day.

3) Successive Intuitive Communication: Each intuitive sense successively communicates intuitive messages—one after the other and in no set order. Bret intuitively hears low rumbling noises. Intuitively tastes lukewarm raindrops. Intuitively speaks about an imminent storm. Intuitively feels a cautious feeling that indicates to carry an umbrella. Intuitively knows to seek solid shelter. Intuitively smells moist wind. Intuitively sings "Stormy Weather." Intuitively sees a flashing inner vision show a murky sky. Bret senses a severe thunderstorm hits his town earlier than meteorologists forecast it.

4) Interconnected Intuitive Communication: Multiple intuitive senses communicate linked intuitive messages at different times. Jannette skates past a local bookstore and intuitively feels excitement in her bones. The next day, in her temporal lobes, she intuitively hears the name of a best selling author she desires to meet. She stops in the bookstore to browse and sees that same author at a book signing. Jannette sensed his bookstore appearance.

5) United Intuitive Communication: Multiple people's intuitive senses communicate intuitive messages, in their own ways, for identical topics or events. Three people are asked the question: What natural disaster will impact the United States? Felicia intuitively sees a rolling inner vision show a 7.8 earthquake strike an east coast city in late October. Dorian intuitively feels falling maple tree leaves touch his feet and the trembling sensations of the city's tallest building. Claire intuitively tastes breezy weather and intuitively speaks, "Crumbling pavement on city streets." They all sense a major earthquake will hit an east coast city during autumn.

Independently or jointly, your intuitive senses keep you moving in the intuitive flow.

---

4. How do I know if I have intuition?

Everyone has intuition. God bestowed this spiritual gift on us all for guidance and protection each day. Intuition isn't limited to special people or a select group, while the rest endure life the best they can.

The main key is to know how your intuition communicates intuitive messages to you; each person is unique. What intuitively works for you could prove ineffective for someone else and vice versa.

Loren intuitively tastes sage honey spicing her new personal relationship. Jack intuitively feels a tickling sensation for the latest lady in his life. Monica intuitively hears a romantic song express her recent union. In unique ways, each person's intuition communicates a similar intuitive message: a loving individual entered her or his life.

Recall how many times you intuitively dreamed of an event that happened within a week. Intuitively felt a hunch regarding a relative's crime that proved true. Intuitively heard real versus fictional stories. Intuitively knew how to save a life during a highway accident. Intuitively tasted spoiled food before ordering it. Intuitively smelled the direction to drive to a new business without reading a map or GPS. Intuitively spoke the unheard ending of a funny story. Intuitively sang an improvised song that uplifted your spirit.

You have eight intuitive senses (see Question 2) at varying levels of development. Two to four intuitive senses communicate intuitive messages to you most of the time.

You're born with intuition living inside you.
It's your spiritual gift to use each day.

---

5. How do I know when I have intuitive experiences?

Intuitive experiences are your direct spiritual encounters with things seen and unseen—often unexplainable by scientific measures. You participate in countless spiritual encounters happening in the spirit realm before or while they occur in the physical realm. Sometimes it feels as though you march on the backdrop of *The Twilight Zone* and land a starring role in weekly episodes.

Intuitive experiences occur anytime and anywhere. Ways to know you have intuitive experiences are when you:

- Speak intuitive expressions true to events.
- Detect things invisible to your physical senses.
- Sense mystical things no one else notices.
- Attribute perceived insights to your wild imagination.
- Receive prophecies fulfilled the same day or later.
- Wonder how you know details with no prior knowledge.
- Doubt truths that, at first, seem improbable or weird.
- Discern secret information you wish to forget.
- Watch a program or movie and sense what happens next.
- Feel uneasy or frightened while hearing eerie noises.
- Feel curious or crazy while hearing ghostly voices.

- Witness mystifying past, present, and future events.
- Awaken and sense otherworldly activities.
- Receive spiritual visits from deceased loved ones.

INTUITIVE SIGNALS

Intuitive signals sometimes alert you to intuitive experiences before or while they occur. Signals include light or color flashes, prickly or tingling sensations, clicking or drumming sounds, perfumed or odorous scents, and smooth or abrasive tastes. They grab your attention despite what you're doing, including while you travel toward or enter a dangerous zone obscuring a harmful person, place, or thing.

For example, you walk into a grocery store. You intuitively hear a shrill siren. Then an angelic voice warns, "Be careful. Slippery floor on Aisle 11." No "slippery floor" signs are posted, but you tiptoe up that aisle.

Other intuitive signals include head pressure, eye twitching, nose or hand itching, lip quivering, and sudden anxiety having no medical, meteorological, or environmental basis. They stop once you become aware of the signals or discover the reasons.

If your intuitive signals are imperceptible, tell your intuition to communicate and intensify two or three signals at least five seconds prior to your intuitive experiences transpiring. Or choose your own intuitive signals so you'll know what to expect. Simply tell your intuition to communicate, for instance, a fantastic feeling, trumpet blast, or lollipop taste. Then notice your intuitive experiences.

PRESENT AND PAST INTUITIVE MOMENTS

Focus on present moments to identify intuitive experiences in progress. Sense when your attention, mood, or reality shifts and why. Be prepared to act, if necessary. Intuitive experiences can occur instantly like newsflashes.

Jermaine undergoes an intuitive experience. He intuitively knows to check on his thirteen-year-old daughter at school; neither she nor a school official phoned him. He stops working and calls the school's main office to validate his intuitive knowing. The principal states, "Your daughter is sick and needs to go home."

Focus on past moments to identify intuitive experiences after they have occurred. Have you intuitively seen visions or dreams show innovative medical technologies? Intuitively felt on target or off target while making composite decisions? Intuitively heard modern poetry recited after everyone left a room? Intuitively known where to find grammatical errors in newspaper articles? Intuitively tasted thorny flavors alerting you to safety or danger? Intuitively smelled peppery scents conveying fortune or misfortune? Intuitively spoken blissful affirmations to the downhearted? Intuitively sung songs uncovering transportation problems?

EVOLUTION OF INTUITIVE EXPERIENCES

Intuitive experiences happening to you today and in the future will evolve from those that occurred yesteryear. Intuition development is a lifelong educational process. You learn about it and recognize it and grow. You experiment with it and live it and advance.

For example, two years ago, you intuitively saw visions and dreams show events happening to loved ones in this life. Today, you intuitively see visions and dreams show events happening to loved ones in the afterlife. Next year, you'll communicate intuitive messages between loved ones in this life and in the afterlife.

It takes time to adjust to the evolution of your intuitive experiences and modify your beliefs about how intuition works. Just when you think you know it all, extraordinary intuitive experiences occur. At times, it feels as if you rocket out of your body and into other spiritual dimensions beyond earth's gravitational pull. Spend time out in nature to keep yourself grounded. Go walking, hiking, picnicking, camping, surfing, or sailing.

Intuitive experiences shape your life management skills.

MONEY-SAVING FEELING

I drove my car to a service center in Northern Virginia. In my bones, I intuitively felt certain the squeaking engine noise cost less to repair than the $240 a manager estimated. I was having an intuitive experience. I knew little about auto mechanics but refused to accept his deliberate overcharge.

"Can I drive my car another week without causing a problem?" I asked.

"Yes," he mumbled, shuffling papers.

I left the service center and drove to an auto repair shop a friend recommended. The owner had integrity. I paid $20 for a simple engine belt adjustment. My intuitive feeling saved me $220. I recognized how I sensed overcharges. That service center lost a customer.

6. Do I need to meditate to use my intuition?

Meditation holds different meanings for different people. In general, it involves calming your mind and emotions and being conscious of your inner state in the present moment. Meditation is valuable when you start using your intuition or when you experience difficulty paying attention to it.

During meditation, focus on your breaths or heartbeats. Let mental chatter and emotional surges come and go. Attempts to silence them amplify them and waste your time. Meditate with or without playing music, lighting candles, or burning incense. Close your eyes or leave them open. Sit, stand, walk, jog, or dance. How regularly you meditate per week is up to you. Five to thirty minutes each time is adequate for using your intuition.

Meditate in quiet places: churches, libraries, and parks. Meditate in noisier places: restaurants, stadiums, and nightclubs. You perfect tuning out surrounding sounds and sensing your inner guidance that imparts information and answers your questions for different areas of life. In time, you use your intuition with or without meditating wherever you are. Here's a useful meditation technique:

Sit, relax, and close your eyes.
Take a deep breath and hold it for three seconds.
Exhale it for three seconds.

Now imagine that you enter a sacred room.
The room is filled with shining gold light.
The light enters your heart and expands.
It moves up past your head three inches.
It moves down below your feet three inches.
Feel your inner power.

Ask your intuition a question.
Sense the answer from one or multiple intuitive senses.
Feel the truth of it.
When you're ready, exit the room.
Leave the door open so that you can go there anytime.
The light stays with you and shines forever.

Take a deep breath and hold it for three seconds.
Exhale it for three seconds.
Open your eyes.

Additional meditation techniques are available in metaphysical books in bookstores, via meditation classes, and on websites. For the latter, use an Internet search engine and separately type in the words "meditation," "meditation techniques," and "meditation exercises." Use techniques suitable for you or create your own.

Meditate and listen for inner guidance.

---

7. Can tools or rituals help me use my intuition?

Metaphysical tools and rituals help you use your intuition. They function as extensions of your intuitive senses and provide outer mirrors reflecting your inner world. Tools and rituals work because you believe they do. Your beliefs give them inward-to-outward power.

Metaphysical tools aid you in answering your questions. Such tools include astrology, numerology, runes, pendulums, crystals, and cards. Use simple or multipart charts and layouts.

Roberta asks, "Why can't I remember my dreams?" She completes a three-card layout revealing religious dogma blocks her dream recall. A second layout reveals a way to re-program her religious beliefs before falling asleep.

Rituals are repetitious ceremonial actions or procedures. They're performed for distinct purposes: activate spiritual gifts, increase intuitive knowledge, promote physical healing—and so on.

Mitzi dances for ten minutes every Friday and intuitively speaks natural remedies for health problems. She successfully tests skin care remedies on family and friends.

Use tools and rituals as you desire. However, everything you need to use your intuition already lives within you. Each day, pay attention to your intuitive visions, dreams, feelings, sensations, sounds, knowings, tastes, scents, sayings, and songs.

Bernard intuitively hears a lively radio jingle. It solves a relationship issue he mulls before exploring his astrological chart for planetary alignments and aspects. Nikita intuitively knows the information explaining her streak of good fortune prior to her chanting to obtain the reason.

During time-critical events, you have little or no time to reach for a tool or perform a ritual. Traffic accidents, household injuries, and physical attacks can hit you like lightning strikes. Yet, your intuition guides and protects you in advance when you act on its guidance.

Intuitive knowledge comes from within you.
No tools or rituals are required.

SNAKE ON A NATURE TRAIL

Several friends and I hiked in beautiful Cloudland Canyon, in Rising Fawn, Georgia. Three hours later, we approached a nature trail's ending. In my temporal lobes, I intuitively heard a keen voice yell, "Look down!"

I had no time to reach for a tool or perform a ritual to determine why I needed to look down. I saw a petite black snake crawl on the trail five feet ahead. Poisonous or harmless, I kept a safe distance and watched it crawl out of sight.

8. What are literal and symbolic messages?

Intuitive messages are literal, symbolic, or both. Literal intuitive messages retain original meanings and require no interpretations. Overanalyzing them results in inaccuracies. For example, a shining light bulb means your glowing ceiling light.

Symbolic intuitive messages are multifaceted and require accurate interpretations. Misapprehending them results in errors. For example, a shining light bulb represents your spiritual radiance.

Some intuitive messages are literal and symbolic. Literal elements require no interpretations, unlike symbolic elements. For example, an open door to an office building literally means your workplace. It leads to a second open door and into a remodeled hospital operating room symbolizing your new way of operating in your workplace.

Symbols represent life's vast subjects: a framed picture represents trapped coal miners (people), fenced homes (places), enclosed ideas (things), and confined marriages (situations). Symbols also represent intangibles: a red heart for eternal love, a pointed arrow for a focused mind, and a dirty blanket for impure air.

Three common types of symbols are:

1) Personal symbols are based on your life experiences, including inherent and acquired knowledge, talents, and skills. A police officer represents a protector and justice to one person but a menace and injustice to someone else wrongfully arrested for a crime.

2) Cultural symbols are based on the history, customs, and beliefs of people and their environment. A monument, flag, or tattoo holds diverse meanings for different cultures.

3) Universal symbols are shared by everyone, regardless of gender, race, culture, doctrine, or religion. Water universally represents birth, emotions, and spirituality.

Ask your intuition, "What are my symbols? How are they used in my intuitive messages?" Sense the intuitive answers. Record them in your intuition dictionary (see Question 9).

Literal and symbolic intuitive messages broaden your intuitive experiences in meaningful ways.

THE JET SKIER

"How is my day going to flow?" I ask my intuition one morning before driving to work.

I intuitively see a rolling inner vision show a jet skier gliding on smooth waters. Though I have never driven a jet ski, my intuition uses my observations of jet skiers as a personal symbol representing how my day will flow.

Smooth waters symbolize an easy day; rough waters, a harsh day. A straight run symbolizes normal activities; a quick turn in another direction, abrupt changes.

If my day tosses challenges, I ask my intuition, "What can I do to have a good day, anyway?" I listen for inner guidance and act on it. I'm often guided to set my intent for and affirm, "Peace and productivity."

9. Why does intuition communicate using symbols?

Symbols are a part of your soul's language and speak volumes when words alone are insufficient. They grab your attention and inform you about someone or something. Each symbol represents multiple words containing compound meanings. Sensing a symbol's correct meaning each time you receive a symbolic intuitive message is essential. Your intuitive senses, except for intuitive knowing, communicate symbolic intuitive messages in unlimited ways.

A symbol tells a story pertaining to the past, present, or future. Because of differing backgrounds, each person has special personal and cultural symbols, though similar situations occur. Each person interprets symbolic intuitive messages based on his or her life's experiences—birth to adulthood.

A stove represents a cooking appliance to Todd, a heater to Fantasia, and a dangerous device to Millicent. In symbolic intuitive messages, Todd interprets the stove to mean a way to cook up ideas for family fun. Fantasia interprets it to mean a need to heat her cold personality. Millicent interprets it to mean a former friend attempts to burn her good reputation.

SERIAL SYMBOLS

Serial symbols transpire in intuitive messages. Their meanings remain unchanged or switch.

Walter intuitively dreams he catches fish in a lake. The next night, he hooks fish on a wet hilltop. On the third night, he nets fish from a moist rainbow. His "catching fish" serial symbol remains unchanged and represents his desire to break away from his nerve-racking career and enjoy an outdoor activity.

Debbie intuitively hears her brother's inner voice say, "Goodbye, my blend." It represents the end of his smoking addiction. The next time she intuitively hears his inner voice, his words switch meaning and represent him giving away his mixed-breed puppy.

A serial symbol can rework its characteristics in intuitive messages. Again, its meaning remains unchanged or switches.

Maggie suffers a viral infection and intuitively tastes the top of a sewing needle. Its small opening represents minor health improvement. In her second intuitive message, the needle's wider opening represents major health improvement. In her third intuitive message, its huge opening represents total recovery.

Ask your intuition, "What are my serial symbols?" Sense the intuitive answers. Record them in your intuition dictionary.

SWITCHING SYMBOLS

Symbols can switch meanings per intuitive message. Your intuition uses symbols in ways that best communicate your soul's language with infinite scenarios and endings.

Loren intuitively dreams she drives on a dusty road and encounters a male hitchhiker thumbing for a ride. Her dream occurs three times in a week. In her first dream, the hitchhiker represents an associate expecting a free ride to work every day. In her second dream, he represents an impulsive trip to a cooperative town. In her third dream, he represents a risky investment to bypass.

Ask your intuition, "What are my switching symbols?" Sense the intuitive answers. Record them in your intuition dictionary.

INTUITION DICTIONARY

Follow the guidance provided in Question 10 to learn how to interpret your symbolic intuitive messages. Create an intuition dictionary—paper or computerized—capturing your personal, cultural, and universal symbols and meanings, along with literal meanings. Your dictionary expands throughout your life.

Note the example entries:

> *Ant.* Literal: ant. Symbolic: diligence, loyalty, antsy feeling, petty thing, pun on aunt.

> *Garden.* Literal: garden. Symbolic: nurturer, beauty, potential, inner growth.

SHARING INTUITIVE MESSAGES

Sense when to share literal, symbolic, and literal/symbolic intuitive messages, when to keep details hidden from cynical, gossipy or vindictive people, and when to avert upsetting or frightening others.

Mike wants to disclose his angelic encounters with a friend. He intuitively feels a resistant feeling that indicates his friend will ridicule him. Georgette intuitively smells a deadly scent around her personal trainer and tells him. The scent represents his spiritual transformation, not the physical death he fears.

Flexibility and patience are required to understand
the intricacies of intuitive messages.

SWITCHING BABY

In my intuitive messages, a baby is one of my switching symbols. Depending on an intuitive message's structure, he or she represents a new project, a wise messenger, an unfed talent, or an immature adult. I must accurately interpret the baby's meaning each time to understand the intuitive message communicated to me.

10. How do I interpret symbolic intuitive messages?

Accurate interpretation is required to obtain the true meanings of symbolic intuitive messages. The interpretation process is an inherent or a learned ability.

Start with willingness, patience, and an open mind. Release beliefs about what each symbol represents per intuitive message; meanings can switch. Notice the images, sounds, tastes, scents, conversations, and actions in each intuitive message. Grasp how you feel—from beginning to end—in the represented area of life.

Give each intuitive message a short title: *Spider Hanging on a Red Ledge*, *Twelfth Floor Elevator*, or *Love Affair in Dallas*. A title captures the fundamental nature of the theme.

Two techniques to interpret symbolic intuitive messages are:

1) The Prayer Technique. Pray to God for divine understanding and expect to receive the interpretation via one or multiple intuitive senses. Each symbol's meaning flows or pops into your awareness.

2) The Questioning Technique. Ask each symbol one of the following questions: What are you telling me? What do you mean? What do I need to understand? What's your truth? One or multiple intuitive senses communicate the interpretation to you.

Prayer and questioning give you the power to
interpret symbolic intuitive messages.

THE CORPORATE PITCHER

During a message circle, I intuitively saw a rolling inner vision show a man pitching baseballs to batters who hit them out of the ballpark. He switched pitches and they hit foul or catchable balls. The batters, along with spectators sitting on bleachers, became angry.

I gave my symbolic intuitive message a concise title: *The Pitcher Finds His Way Home*. I intuitively felt a strong feeling indicate the man reviled his career and hungered to live his life purpose. I used the questioning technique to interpret my intuitive message about him.

"What are you telling me?" I asked my intuition, discerning the baseball game and pitcher both represented a gifted young man participating in the message circle.

In my inner ear, I intuitively heard my inner voice reply, "As long as he works the way his colleagues insist, they're thrilled—home run hitters. When he works his way, they complain—losers."

The man stated, "I plan to pursue an entertainment career and quit my terrible corporate job." In the movie industry, he'd fulfill his life purpose.

I interpreted my inner vision as illustrating how his changed career plans (switched pitches) angered his colleagues (batters and spectators). Their jobs became difficult to perform (foul or catchable balls) without him (a once accommodating pitcher) leading the way.

11. Why should I use my intuition?

Use your intuition because it guides and protects you seven days a week. How many times has logic failed you? How often have intuitive experiences baffled common sense? Have you experienced a life-impacting situation and sighed, "If only I'd known"? Your intuition ensures you know in twenty-eight areas of life:

Animals and Insects	Objects
Business Management	Other People
Career	Politics
Divine Communication	Property
Education	Relationships
Family and Friends	Science and Technology
Finances	Spiritual Growth
Food and Beverage	Spirit Realm
Geology and Weather	Sports and Entertainment
Health	Talents and Gifts
Ideas and Inventions	Time Management

Law and Justice	Transportation
Life Purpose	Travel
Nature and Environment	World News

Have you sensed an unknown talent, a health misdiagnosis, or a travel opportunity? Have you sensed a creative idea, political win, or geological event? Your intuition, automatically or by request, communicates these matters and more.

DOUBLE VALIDATION FOR PEANUTS

"What food am I allergic to right now?" I asked my intuition, while relaxing at home one evening. A TV commercial played in the background.

In my temporal lobes, I intuitively heard a solitary word "peanuts." Then I physically heard a TV commercial's character twice utter, "Peanuts." The commercial, unrelated to my question, supplied double validation.

I had experienced stomach irritation after consuming peanuts but saw no visible reactions: skin rashes, throat tightening, or facial swelling. Medical tests reported no peanut allergy. My gift of intuitive hearing answered my question for two areas of life: food and health.

INTUITION BENEFITS

"How does it benefit me to use my intuition?" people ask. It's a valid question that changes lives once the continual impact is understood. Every time you heed your intuition, note how it helped you. Every time you ignore your intuition, note how it would have helped you if you had acted on its guidance. Use your intuition and reap twenty-one benefits:

- Discern things about yourself and others.
- Make wise and timely decisions.
- Manage diverse personalities and situations.
- Predict future events and discoveries.
- Uncover erroneous or missing data.
- Sense problems and solutions in advance.
- Sense success or failure ahead of time.
- Know to wait, proceed, or stop.
- Know to speak or remain silent.
- Locate missing people, animals, or objects.
- Save or increase time, money, and energy.
- Detect hidden health issues.
- Handle corrupt legal or political issues.
- Perceive deception or danger.
- Handle positive and negative energies.
- Understand spirit realm communication.
- Protect or save a life.
- Sense opportunities and revelations.
- Sense what's changeable and unchangeable.
- Recognize your calling or purpose in life.
- Know everything will be all right.

Your intuition watches over you at home and on the go.

POLICE RADAR DETECTION

I drove to an afternoon business meeting on Interstate 85 in Georgia. I intuitively saw a flashing inner vision show a male police officer positioned to issue tickets to speeding drivers. I glanced at hotspots but saw no patrol car or motorcycle.

I decreased my driving speed below the posted limit. I glanced up at an overpass two seconds before driving underneath it. I spotted several police officers pointing radar guns at drivers and knew everything would be all right for me. I saved time (officer interaction), money (a $150 speeding ticket), and energy (ticket frustration).

12. How do I trust my intuition?

You trust your intuition once you realize how relieved, peaceful, or contented you'd feel if you had listened to and acted on the intuitive messages you received about someone or something. Hindsight appreciates nowsight and foresight.

Hindsight is understanding an intuitive experience after it happens. Nowsight is grasping an intuitive experience while it happens. Foresight is knowing an event before it happens.

Have you sensed to discard a diary product ahead of its expiration date, go to the bathroom though you waited, or avoid answering a phone call from a friend? What happened when you distrusted your intuition? Did you suffer a stomachache from eating spoiled eggs, worry the occupied bathroom increased your wait time, or tolerate an annoying conversation? These incidents and others are averted as soon as you trust your intuition and act on its guidance.

Many intuitive experiences occur every day. Practice trusting your intuition for small events in your life. Then trust it for significant events. You can decide to do things your way, other people's way, or the intuitive way. Your intuition never forces you to act as guided.

You have free will—the freedom to make wise or unwise choices for any situation. But when you become upset, fed up, or exhausted from undesirable outcomes, such as preventable injuries, wasted finances, or crumbling relationships, you discover the intuitive way is the best way.

Examples: Trusting and Distrusting Intuition

Intuitive Seeing: Charlie intuitively sees a paused outer vision show an ex-girlfriend continuing her verbal abuse. He heeds his intuition and refuses to answer her apologetic phone calls.

Intuitive Feeling: Mona's cousins ask her to help them move furniture. She intuitively feels a resistant feeling but disregards it. Afterward, she feels used and unappreciated.

Intuitive Hearing: Tony considers marrying his childhood sweetheart and intuitively hears applause. Later, their happy marriage produces two sons and a daughter.

Intuitive Knowing: Jean intuitively knows to call her ailing grandma. She procrastinates and her grandma suffers a fatal heart attack.

Intuitive Tasting: Symms talks to next-door neighbors and pays attention to the numerical relish she intuitively tastes. She invests in their future multi-million dollar franchise.

Intuitive Smelling: Steven dances in a nightclub. He intuitively smells a fading plastic scent but ignores it. He loses his driver's license.

Intuitive Speaking: Omni intuitively speaks, "I'll stop at the new department store on my way home." She receives a $100 gift certificate for being the 100th customer.

Intuitive Singing: Chris intuitively sings, "Cracked sidewalk under my sandals." He dismisses the lyrics, until he stumbles and falls.

In trusting your intuition, you trust yourself.

Store Product Alert

I began to trust my intuition through recurring intuitive experiences. Like movie reruns, my intuition alerted me to desired products shelved in stores I entered to buy other items. I'd planned to drive to other stores to buy those products. I intuitively saw a flashing inner vision show a product and its store section. Or in my temporal lobes, I intuitively heard a gentle voice say, "It's here."

My logic disagreed. "No way it's here," I said and left the store. My fatigue increased from running in and out of stores. Eventually, I surrendered and said, "Why not? Let me check." I had nothing to lose.

In my body, I intuitively felt a tingling sensation or nervousness the closer I moved near the section where my intuition guided me. I found the product I desired. Trusting my intuition repeatedly saved me driving time, vehicle wear, and gas money.

13. How do I act on intuitive messages I receive?

Each intuitive message contains guidance on how to act. You sense what to say or do, though you may desire to perform other actions.

Have you sensed to listen to a bird sing to let it brighten your day? Sensed to drive pass a pharmacy to have a prescription filled cheaper elsewhere? Sensed to go for a walk to improve your body's blood circulation? Did you listen to or ignore your intuition for those situations or others? You have two choices: follow your inner guidance or not. The latter brings consequences, which may take days, months, or years to normalize or live through.

Leeann chops apples in her kitchen and intuitively feels the cutting sensation of a knife on her left hand. She doubts her intuition until she nicks her middle finger. Quincy rides a commuter bus and intuitively knows to chat with an elderly woman. He continues gazing out a window and misses cheering up the recent widow. Brenda intuitively speaks, "Skip kick boxing." Instead, she prances and leaves the gym feeling piercing back pain.

The type of intuitive message you receive determines the time to act. Recognize non-urgent intuitive messages, for instance, unread emails, forgotten groceries, and unshredded papers. You have hours or days to act. Recognize urgent intuitive messages, for instance, exclusive opportunities, health crises, and destructive earthquakes. You have seconds or minutes to act.

The more you use your inner guidance every day, the easier it is to act on your intuitive messages as guided. You stop regrettably saying, "I'll tend to that later," or "It won't happen."

Timely intuitive actions lead to satisfying outcomes.

DVD FOR SALE

After shopping at a local mall, I considered driving to an electronics retail store to buy the movie *The Mothman Prophecies*. In my stomach, I intuitively felt a sinking feeling that indicated the movie's DVD wasn't available in the retail store.

Then I intuitively felt a strong feeling that indicated to stop in a video rental store. I doubted a purchasable copy existed. I acted on my inner guidance, stopped in the store, and bought the sole DVD lying on a shelf.

14. Is intuition always right?

Intuition is always right. It communicates nothing except the truth. Overanalyzing a literal intuitive message or misinterpreting a symbolic intuitive message leads to a false conclusion that your intuition is wrong. And you doubt or ignore an intuitive message when it defies logic, contradicts your physical senses, clashes with a desire, or presents a new situation for you.

Have you doubted an intuitive message about despicable people because they seemed polite or righteous? Rejected an intuitive message describing untidy beach resorts while scanning flawless magazine pictures parading them? Ignored an intuitive message foretelling a heartbreak after you prayed it away? If so, what resulted?

Review your intuitive journal or recall your intuitive experiences. In your mind, replay your actions regarding the intuitive messages you received and the outcomes. Determine why you believed your intuition was wrong when it proved right.

Your intuition communicates unchanging truth.
Mental and emotional versions alter the truth.

BUMPS AND SPILLS

I set an eight-ounce drinking glass containing water on a kitchen countertop. I intuitively saw a flashing inner vision show my arm knocking over the glass. Since I'd set it on the countertop's center, I doubted my intuition.

As I removed a carton of milk from my refrigerator, my right elbow bumped the glass. Water spilled on the countertop and floor. I cleaned up the spill and knew I should have listened to my inner guidance.

I recognized my intuition warned me when I bordered on knocking over a container filled with a liquid, gel, or powder. My intuitive warnings contradicted my physical observations: My arm won't hit the container. My leg won't kick it. No object will fall on it.

Now I reposition containers and pay attention while moving around them once I receive intuitive warnings about bumps and spills. The warnings save me frustration and clean-up time.

15. How do I know what my intuition tells me is real?

Validations let you know what your intuition communicates is real. In time, you receive undeniable proof that silences logic.

Eve intuitively dreams she passes a college psychology exam. It comes true two days later, though failing self-talk had hounded her. Ken intuitively feels a deflated feeling that indicates a flat truck tire. It happens the next week despite a visual inspection. Sara intuitively tastes lemon wedding cake. Her friend and lemon cake lover, Bradley, pledges bachelorhood but marries within a year.

Investigate intuitive messages involving the past to know what's real. Review courthouse records, browse Internet sites, and contact those knowledgeable of earlier times.

Ally intuitively dreams she holds a black and white photograph of an unknown paternal great-great grandfather. She phones her paternal grandparents. They describe his facial features identical to what she saw in her intuitive dream.

Follow through for intuitive messages related to the present. Pursue a hunch, interpret a dream, or heed a knowing.

Russ intuitively knows a crowded parking lot contains an empty space beyond his physical eyesight. He drives to the row containing the empty space.

Play a waiting game for intuitive messages concerning the future. Monitor news reports, attend cutting-edge conventions, and listen to visionary discussions.

On a sunny Wednesday afternoon, Maria intuitively feels a watery sensation rise to her knees. On a rainy Sunday evening, TV weather reports show knee-high water flooding her town's streets.

What about mind-boggling intuitive experiences? Animals talk to you. You astral travel to foreign countries. Deceased relatives visit you. Validate those intuitive experiences, too. Do the animals reveal a truth about your life? Can you match astral travel scenery to travel brochures for those countries? Do your loved ones give you accurate intuitive messages for yourself and others?

Intuitive experiences are validated—today or later.

VEHICLE ACCIDENT WARNING

I washed my face in my bathroom sink. I intuitively saw a rolling inner vision show the grieving face of a young cousin who drowned in a lake in the 1980s. I wondered why. Then I intuitively saw a second rolling inner vision show his younger brother driving in Nashville, Tennessee. Inattentive, he crashed into a telephone pole. Blood splattered everywhere. My deceased cousin wanted me to warn his brother about his deadly driving habit.

Are these visions real? I asked myself. *Did my cousin visit me while I washed my face? Was his brother inattentive while driving?* I last saw him in 2002. I intuitively felt an urgent feeling in my spirit. I called their older sister, my best friend.

"My mother told him to pay attention to the highway while he's driving," she gasped. "She's afraid he'll have a bad accident."

I gasped, too, realizing my imagination wasn't tricking me. My deceased cousin's intuitive warning proved real. My best friend delivered my intuitive message to their younger brother.

16. Can I question my intuition about any life situation?

Intuition By Request (IBR) is an easy three-step process for you to question your intuition about any life situation and sense accurate intuitive answers. No thinking or wishing is necessary. Ask questions generating "yes or no" or "in-depth" answers. The IBR process includes the following steps:

1) Clarify your question. Spell out what you truly want to know and understand. One or multiple intuitive senses will communicate an accurate answer. Suspend your doubts and fears to prevent blocking or ignoring the answer.

2) Ask your question during a quiet or hectic moment while you're ready and receptive. Sustain an unshakable knowing that the answer you seek will materialize. It exists in your "inner space" awaiting your awareness. Detach from what you think the answer is or desire it to be. Remain open to unlimited possibilities.

3) Sense the intuitive answer. Know which of the intuitive senses communicate the answer—literal, symbolic, or literal/symbolic—in response to your question. An accurate answer intuitively feels right or on target. Act on the inner guidance you receive. The validation is instant or comes later.

Clarify → Ask → Sense

Jeri clarifies her question and then asks her intuition, "What's the best career path for me?" She intuitively sees a flashing inner vision show her acting in a theater play. She hasn't considered a career in the performing arts but has dwelled on chemical engineering. She attends acting classes to validate it's her best career path.

Common questions people ask their intuition include:

- What's my life purpose?
- Where can I find a good job?
- Will I find a loving man (or woman)?
- How do I save my marriage?
- What's bothering my child?
- How can I better manage my time?
- Do I have enemies?
- Why is this diet plan useless?
- Where is the best place to vacation this year?
- Can I succeed running my own business?

Practice asking your intuition questions and sensing the intuitive answers each day. Start with things you consider secondary in your life to stroll into the intuitive flow. Then include things you deem primary. Ask additional questions, for every subject, to gain greater knowledge and understanding. You aren't limited to one question per situation or per day. However, repeatedly asking the same question allows your ego or logic to respond with a more convincing answer. You might reject the intuitive answer that's correct. Such rejections cause you to live your life opposing the intuitive way.

Intuitive questioning and answering put you in charge
of your life. You're a follower and a leader.

17. How can I use my intuition every day?

Decide to use your intuition every day in numerous areas of life (see Question 11). Know how, when, and where your intuitive senses communicate intuitive messages to you. Listen for soft and loud intuitive knocks. Allow insights to come to you without judgment or rejection. Then trust and act on your intuitive messages. In time, you recognize your intuitive style. Remember, your intuitive senses communicate independently or jointly, switch between intuitive messages, and alternate literally and symbolically.

The intuitive messages you receive are related or unrelated to your current activity. Notice if they drop in, for instance, while you brush your hair, tidy your bed, talk with your sibling, feed a pet, drive to work, study for an exam, or perform a hobby.

On Thursday, Nichole loads flatware in her dishwasher. She intuitively hears her inner voice warn, "Carefully load steak knives." Her intuitive message, related to her current activity, protects her from a physical injury. On Sunday, she loads flatware in her dishwasher. She intuitively feels a rushing sensation indicate to stop and watch local news. Her intuitive message, unrelated to her current activity, allows her to witness a news reporter questioning her brave uncle who detained a house burglar wielding a meat cleaver.

INTUITION BY REQUEST

Ask your intuition questions throughout the day. Divide your questioning and answering (Q&A) sessions by day and night or by morning, afternoon, and evening. Maintain an unshakable knowing that you'll sense the intuitive answers. They reside in your "inner space" awaiting your awareness. Ask follow-up questions to obtain greater knowledge and understanding of your intuitive answers. Act on the inner guidance you receive.

Andre asks his intuition, "Why am I always tired?" He intuitively speaks, "Inadequate rest." He's surprised because he sleeps seven to eight hours each night. Following up, he asks his intuition, "Why do I need adequate rest?" He intuitively hears the loud clicking sound of his TV switch on. His intuition advises him to turn off his noisy TV at bedtime, to wake up well rested.

Common questions to ask your intuition every day include:

- How will my day flow?
- What should I eat for breakfast?
- Who unexpectedly calls me?
- Why do I feel an urge to email a friend?
- Am I forgetting something I need to do?
- Why should I take a break now?
- How do I resolve a family issue?
- Does an opportunity exist for me to pursue?
- How can I increase my energy?
- Will I encounter travel delays?

Journal your intuitive answers, including the wild, scary, and tragic ones. They communicate insights, too. Your intuition uses "everything" you've seen, felt, heard, and done throughout your lifetime and incorporates it in your intuitive messages to guide and protect you. "Everything" includes classroom activities, dating antics, family matters, work incidents, vacation habits, and radio songs. Validate the intuitive messages you receive.

You sense a less complicated life in each day's reality.
You live an easier life by listening to your intuition.

IS THIS PLANE GOING TO CRASH?

I boarded an airplane at a Memphis, Tennessee airport. I intuitively felt throat tightness indicate "something is wrong with this plane."

"Is this plane going to crash?" I asked my intuition.

"No," replied a direct voice I intuitively heard in my inner ear.

How weird, I thought. *Why do I feel tightness in my throat if this plane is okay?* I boarded the airplane. It remained at the gate for an hour, while mechanics attempted to repair flawed equipment. They diagnosed it unusable but non-essential. The captain disabled it.

"Is this plane going to crash?" I asked my intuition.

"No," replied a gentle voice I intuitively heard in my inner ear, as the captain allowed terrified passengers to deboard the plane.

My throat tightness disappeared. We landed safely at Dulles Airport in Herndon, Virginia. In hindsight, I realized my mind grabbed the worst-case ending. I didn't ask my intuition the right question: "What's wrong with this airplane?"

18. Why are some people more intuitive than others?

Spiritually, nobody is more intuitive than anybody else. Anyone can sense the truth about people, places, things, and situations. Some people's intuition is further developed than others due to six reasons: awareness, naturally gifted, intuition development habits, family support, open-minded religious beliefs, and confronted fears.

1) Awareness: Some people are aware they have intuition and use it each day; others are unaware and doubt or ignore their intuitive messages. They rely on reasoning or common sense. If they cultivate intuition development habits, they harness the power of intuition. If not they accept the limitations of logic, physical appearances, and prior knowledge.

2) Naturally Gifted: Some people are naturally gifted at using their intuition, just as some are naturally gifted at playing musical instruments, delivering dynamic speeches, or resolving mathematic equations. Each person is born with intuition functioning at varying levels anchored in his or her spiritual missions. Those who aren't naturally gifted cultivate intuition development habits. If not, they allow themselves to be intuitively left behind.

3) Intuition Development Habits: People with a highly developed intuition continually:

- Read intuition books and articles.
- Attend or teach intuition development classes.
- Share intuitive experiences with others.
- Perform intuitive experiments independently or with groups.
- Use their intuition every day.
- Know how, when, and where intuitive experiences occur.
- Distinguish between evolving and new intuitive experiences.
- Record, track, and validate intuitive experiences in a journal.

4) Family Support: Some people have family members who use their intuition in public or private ways. In those familiies, each generation passes down stories and customs to the next generations. Family support instills intuitive knowledge, wisdom, and conviction. People without family support, including dear souls who experience ridicule and abuse from using their intuitive senses, can still possess a highly developed intuition. They keep their natural giftedness or cultivate intuition development habits.

5) Open-Minded Religious Beliefs: Some people's religious beliefs view intuition as being unreal, granted to a select few, or pure evil. Your intuition is as genuine as your breath of life. God granted it to everyone for divine guidance and protection. Anyone who disagrees is uninformed or power hungry. Unlike intuition, pure evil bestows no spiritual gifts to aid your spiritual/human journey. It constructs obstacles and dispenses negativity to dispirit and wound you and others. People with open-minded religious beliefs allow themselves to live in the intuitive flow.

6) Confronted Fears: Some people fear intuition and its insights. They fear the unknown becoming known, invisible spirits chasing them, and information overloads leading to sanity checks. They fear their reactions and responsibilities once they know the truth about someone or something. They do fear other people's reactions toward the usage of their intuition. When people choose to confront, mend, and discharge their fears, they reap all the benefits of listening to and acting on their inner guidance every day.

Intuition—no U-turns back to not knowing the truth.
Being oblivious or in denial ceases to work.

---

19. Why do I have a few intuitive senses?

Everyone has eight intuitive senses at varying development levels. Two to four intuitive senses communicate to you most of the time. Your intuitive senses subtly or dramatically activate at different ages, unless they all turned on at birth. Your spiritual mission determines when it's time for an intuitive sense to activate.

For example, your gift of intuitive tasting activates when you're thirty years old. Your gift guides you in sensing genuine and phony dialogue and deeds occurring in your workplace. Your spiritual mission includes building trusted relationships.

Subtle activations occur, for instance, during prayers, meditations, and massages; dramatic activations occur, for instance, during infirmities, accidents, and assaults. No activation's origin is more superior or spiritual than another's origin. A person whose gift of intuitive hearing activates after suffering whiplash in a car accident is on par with a person whose gift activates after throwing a gutter ball in a bowling alley. A person whose gift of intuitive smelling activates during a surgical procedure is on par with a person whose gift activates while eating donuts. Each individual owns empowering spiritual gifts that are used to improve his or her life and the lives of others.

REQUEST FOR ACTIVATION

If you desire a dormant intuitive sense to activate, make sure you're ready to receive its intuitive communication. Tell your intuition to activate the intuitive sense rather than force its launch. Forcing it leads to questionable or overwhelming intuitive experiences.

For example, you tell your intuition, "Let my gift of intuitive singing come to pass." Be aware when you intuitively sing songs and their meanings. Forcing this gift results in meaningless or sporadic singing. Your higher self, the wise essence of you, delays requests interfering with your highest good. In the meantime, other intuitive senses guide and protect you.

INTUITIVE LIFE REVIEW

Determine if more intuitive senses activated without your awareness. Use my Intuitive Life Review (ILR) strategy to recall your intuitive experiences going as far back as you can remember. This strategy is designed to help you scan your whole life for known, unknown, and forgotten intuitive experiences.

Sit, relax, and take three deep breaths. With your eyes closed or open, focus on your childhood—birth to eighteen years old—for a minute or longer. Focus on your adulthood—nineteen years old to current age—for a minute or longer. Allow memories revealing the usage of your intuitive senses to return to your awareness without analysis or rejection. Thinking and guessing are unnecessary. Notice your intuitive experiences emerge one by one.

Additional intuitive experiences will pop into your awareness in the coming days and weeks, regardless of your activities: shampooing your hair, calculating your expenses, scheduling your weekend, singing in a choir, taking a Pilates class, or talking to a neighbor.

Record your intuitive experiences in your intuitive journal. Examine them to determine which intuitive senses communicated intuitive messages to you. You could discover they all did in the same or different areas of your life. An intuitive sense has activated even if it communicated to you once a week, month, or year. You identified certain intuitive senses more than others because of longtime use.

You intuitively experience bonus tracks.
Look within yourself and replay your intuitive movies.

SPIRITUAL GIFTS IN FULL SWING

I conducted intuitive readings for clients who thought they possessed a few intuitive senses or none. I discovered several clients had the gift of intuitive seeing activated. But they didn't realize they intuitively saw visions while awake and dreams while asleep.

Many clients blocked their gift of intuitive feeling to prevent suffering the world's misery within their human bodies. Others downright rejected their gift of intuitive hearing. They intuitively heard disembodied voices talking and feared institutionalization if people found out.

A few believed their gift of intuitive knowing meant common sense. They just knew stuff and couldn't grasp why others failed to "get the message." The gifts of intuitive tasting, smelling, speaking, and singing remained unknown until I defined them with examples.

"Those experiences did happen," they admitted. "But being intuitive never registered."

20. Are some intuitive senses stronger than others?

No intuitive sense is spiritually stronger than another intuitive sense. Each intuitive sense is capable of communicating intuitive messages to ease and enhance your life. Intuitive seeing, feeling, hearing, and knowing are talked and written about more than intuitive tasting, smelling, speaking, and singing. This creates a false impression: the first group dominates the second group. Be open to receive communication from all eight intuitive senses.

Artis intuitively sees a paused outer vision show water spots on his living room ceiling. Then he intuitively tastes dripping water. He believes his gift of intuitive seeing is stronger than his gift of intuitive tasting because it communicates first and more often. However, both intuitive senses alert him to a leaky roof owing to a busted water pipe and twelve hours before he physically sees it.

Two to four intuitive senses communicate to you the majority of the time. Their frequent use prevails in your life. Be aware of communication from other intuitive senses; their frequent use could prevail. Test it. Say to your intuition, "This week, I'm aware my gifts of <name the intuitive senses> communicate to me more than my gifts of <name the intuitive senses>." Record, track, and validate your intuitive experiences.

Lesser-used intuitive senses capture your attention for playful, routine, and serious reasons. Act on intuitive messages communicated by all intuitive senses.

Marion intuitively hears sounds twenty times greater than she intuitively smells scents. One night, she intuitively smells smoke and her favorite aunt's peach cobbler. Acting on her intuitive message, she calls her aunt who resides 600 miles away. While her aunt and uncle sleep in their bedroom, an unattended coffee maker sparks a fire. Smoke and flames spread. Marion's phone call awakens them. They escape the fire and call 911 from a neighbor's home. Marion's lesser-used gift of intuitive smelling seized her attention and helped her save two lives.

Your intuitive senses hold equal knowledge and power,
no matter how many times you use each of them.

---

21. How does intuition transcend space and time?

In the physical realm, space is a boundless three-dimensional area where people, things, and events shift and have relative position and direction. Time is a measurable linear period during which an action, a process, or a condition begins and continues or ends.

Using your intuition, you possess the power to transcend space and time. All space is sensed as HERE; all time is sensed as NOW. In the spirit and physical realms, you acquire insights about people, places, things, and situations. These insights progress on the space-time grid of centuries and sites, from a physical realm perspective.

Marvin intuitively speaks, "My colleague receives a profitable job offer." His colleague, Fran, works 300 miles outside of headquarters and hides her job search. Two weeks later, she boasts about securing a well-paid job. Marvin's gift of intuitive speaking transcended space (300 miles) and time (two weeks).

At 9:00 AM, Hannah intuitively hears a stern voice warn, "At noon, watch out for the red pickup truck on Interstate 84." The interstate is five miles from her home. Three hours later, she drives to a health spa. She switches lanes to avoid a collision with a red pickup truck driven by a distracted cell phone talker. Her gift of intuitive hearing transcended space (five miles) and time (three hours).

You intuitively travel as an observer and a participant.
What do you sense during your spirit's voyages?

TENNESSEE TORNADOES

In May 2003, I intuitively dreamed tornadoes touched down in a Tennessee county near my sister's home. I phoned her and repeated my intuitive dream. In the afternoon, I watched The Weather Channel and observed a tornado had touched down in her county.

"Did you see that tornado?" I asked my sister, after checking back with her.

"What tornado?" she asked with a surprised tone.

"The one I saw on The Weather Channel," I replied. "Close to where you live."

"Really?" she gasped. "I can sleep through anything."

We laughed. Thankfully, no tornado injured her and other people. I'd intuitively dreamed tornadoes rotated on the ground ten hours before they touched down in Tennessee (time transcended) and 400 miles from my Georgia home (space transcended).

22. Do physical and intuitive senses work together?

Your physical and intuitive senses do work together. Your intuitive senses (unrestricted by space and time) are spiritual extensions for your physical senses (restricted by space and time). For example, your human ears hear within a defined range; your inner ear hears beyond the human range. Each monitors a truth meter.

Renee chats with a cousin in a diner. "Why did Amy accuse you of shoplifting?" she asks him.

"I dumped that immature store clerk," he replies, "and she accused me out of revenge."

She physically hears fifty percent of the truth—he had dated and dumped Amy, the store clerk. The full truth emerges as she intuitively hears his inner voice say, "Amy went on her lunch break while I stole a cashmere sweater. The store manager caught me."

Observing your surroundings with your physical senses allows you to detect additional intuitive messages with your intuitive senses. You sense when someone fells well or ill, when a place is safe or dangerous, when an object is nearby or remote, when an event is routine or abnormal. For example, you observe the hazy white sky. You intuitively feel coldness indicate that the impending snowstorm will be worse than meteorologists predict. Three feet of snow fall versus the forecasted six inches.

Your intuitive senses rise above your physical observations to detect happenings in the spirit realm before they manifest in the physical realm. For example, you intuitively know who'll get married next summer. Your intuitive knowing points to two brides and grooms many people least expect to wed.

Physical and intuitive senses team up to
soften your rational edges.

GUILTY DEFENDANT

As a jurist on a court case, I intuitively knew the defendant stood guilty of the crime accused the moment she walked into the courtroom—no doubt. However, court systems require tangible evidence and eyewitness testimonies, not gut feelings or sudden knowings.

I listened to the plaintiff, two police officers, and the defendant testify. I physically heard her flimsy answers and observed her guilty body language. In my bones, I intuitively felt a funny feeling that indicated her attorney knew she lied. His futile questioning and evidence buried reasonable doubt. Other jurists and I agreed she was guilty based on courtroom proceedings. The case ended in a mistrial.

23. Can logic and intuition work in harmony?

Your logic and intuition work in harmony. Use your intuitive senses for guidance and protection before, during, and after your intuitive experiences wherever you are. Use your logic to analyze your intuitive experiences and understand your intuitive hits and misses.

Opal intuitively tastes grape juice as a healthier morning drink for her than squeezed apple juice. Her logic uses the Internet to analyze the grape juice's antioxidant benefits.

SHADY PARKING TICKET

On a Saturday afternoon, I observed a yellow parking ticket attached to a windshield wiper on my parked car. The police officer knew I had legally parked in a designated area on the Southwest Waterfront in Washington, D.C. I intuitively saw a rolling inner vision show me contesting the shady ticket, though such court cases are tough to win. In my inner ear, I intuitively heard my inner voice advise, "Go there."

Stressed from an unjust job firing, a near-fatal moving accident, and home relocation activities, it would have been easier to pay the ticket via postal mail. But justice demanded its day. I fully read the ticket and saw the wrong day and license plate number written on it. "Go there," my logic agreed.

I dragged myself to court the following Monday and presented my case. I noticed the examiner's dissatisfaction after I'd won. He'd delighted in ruling against four other drivers' cases. I delighted in winning my case and smiled on the inside.

Logic and intuition also work in harmony during intuitive experiences in which logic imparts information.

Joseph trains for a marathon. He intuitively knows how long to exercise each day to prevent serious injuries. If he exercises too long, he intuitively feels tension in his muscles before he physically feels it. His logic reports nutritional facts during his four-month training.

THE STROLLING DOG

I drove on a rural road in Tennessee and spotted a large brown dog sitting on the ground to my left. As my SUV neared the dog, I intuitively knew it would stand and walk into the road.

"Daring animals dash in front of speeding vehicles at the last second," my logic declared.

In my chest, I intuitively felt a strong pushing backward sensation indicate to hit my brakes and come to a stop. The dog stood and then strolled across two lanes to a neighbor's yard. With mulish eyes, it glanced at me to brag, "I'm taking my time. I know you won't hit me."

"Some animals are bolder than others," my logic said.

I intuitively knew that dog sensed I would stop. Animals are intuitive, too.

Sensing and analyzing unite to multiply your wins in life.

---

24. Are intuition and common sense the same?

Your intuition and common sense are disparate gifts. Intuition allows you to sense the truth about people, places, things, and situations from the day you're born. Common sense is defined as natural understanding or sound judgment and is generally based on your life experiences and collective knowledge. Yet, an individual or group can dismiss what's common sense to another individual or group.

Jeremy has the right of way at a pedestrian crosswalk. A taxi driver speeds in his direction. His common sense tells him to wait until the taxi passes by. His common sense is silent while no vehicles are seen or heard racing toward pedestrians, but he intuitively hears a blaring horn warn him to hurry across the crosswalk. A food delivery truck driver races from around an obstructed corner. Acting on his inner guidance, Jeremy remains uninjured.

> Your intuition stays on guard even while
> your common sense is off duty.

25. Why do I ignore my intuition?

To understand why you ignore your intuition, recall your initial reaction while receiving past intuitive messages. Doubt, fear, conflict, and rebellion are the primary drivers.

Did you doubt your intuitive messages carried truth? Did you say, "I'll believe it when I see it"? Your intuitive senses knew information eluding your physical senses. Did you fear ridicule or rejection from yourself and others—fear the truth? Did you devalue intuitive messages conflicting with your desires, your to-do lists, or other people's opinions? Did you rebel against being told what to do, even by your own intuition? Your intuition could have come across as a know-it-all authority figure irritating you.

Christin intuitively feels a tugging feeling that indicates to suspend household chores and drink two glasses of water. She doubts her intuitive message is valid as she doesn't feel thirsty. That afternoon, she ignores her second intuitive message due to a fear of gaining water weight. The next morning, she devalues her third intuitive message. It conflicts with her frenzied caring-for-twins schedule. During the evening, she relaxes with her husband in the family room and resists her fourth intuitive message. "No water for me!" she snaps. Her gift of intuitive feeling warned her four times about her body's dehydration, but her reason for ignoring her gift, viewed as a know-it-all authority figure, varied each time.

Recall what happened after you ignored your intuition. What were your post reactions? Did you laugh or cry? Forgive or criticize yourself? Regret it with a promise to do better?

Today is your day to do better. Step into the intuitive flow. Trust your intuition and act on its guidance. Remember, one intuitive message can transform or save a life.

Examples: Ignoring Intuition

Intuitive Seeing: Marcus intuitively sees a flashing outer vision show four tickets available for a sold-out rock concert. He doubts it and then gripes after an associate buys the extra tickets via the Internet.

Intuitive Feeling: Daphene intuitively feels a resistant feeling that indicates to reject helping a friend pay his cell phone bill. She fears his backlash and lends him $1,250. He refuses to repay her.

Intuitive Hearing: Todd intuitively hears a blues song advising him to forego a blind date his cousin arranged. He believes the song conflicts with what seems to be a harmless tryst, until he meets a nightmarish woman who stalks him.

Intuitive Knowing: Flora intuitively knows to drive on an alternate route to her church. "My normal route is fine," she defies. She drives over large nails left by a construction crew. Her car's front tires deflate and regret agitates her.

Intuitive Tasting: Detrick craves a garden salad he's eaten for years. He intuitively tastes spoiled lettuce but doubts it until eaten lettuce sickens him within two hours.

Intuitive Smelling: Vanica intuitively smells a fresh money scent. She believes her exercise apparatus idea is wasted time and energy. A year later, she observes a stranger capitalizing on the same idea.

Intuitive Speaking: Felix intuitively speaks, "Call my employer at once." Instead, he enjoys his compensatory time off and misses a chance to travel to Switzerland.

Intuitive Singing: Amba intuitively sings, "My mom's coconut cupcakes bore me." She adds cinnamon and nutmeg to her mom's recipe and loses bakery customers.

❊

Invest in yourself. Assert your inner power.

DUMP TRUCK SLAM

While in the Army stationed in Norway in the 1980s, I drove to work one evening. At a green traffic light, I waited for a chance to turn left onto a military base. In my stomach, I intuitively felt a cautious feeling indicate the oncoming dump truck would keep moving after the traffic light turned yellow. I ignored my intuitive feeling; I assumed the truck driver would stop.

I attempted to turn left. The truck slammed into my car on the passenger's side and totaled it. Uninjured, I repeated to myself, "I knew I should have waited a few seconds." I walked or rode the bus to work for months, until I bought another car.

26. Why do I miss my intuitive messages?

You miss your intuitive messages for two reasons: unawareness and faulty expectations. These reasons have adverse effects.

First, you're unaware when you receive intuitive messages. Your attention is diverted elsewhere. For example, you rush to eat lunch and send an inflammatory text message to a friend. Afterward, you realize your intuition communicated an intuitive message alerting you to "check the recipient" prior to hitting the SEND button. You sent the text message to the wrong friend.

Second, your faulty expectations assume intuitive messages will arrive in specific ways. Identify the following variations:

1) Unexpected Intuitive Expression: You expect an intuitive sense to communicate the identical intuitive expression for each intuitive message, but the intuitive expression switches without giving you notice. Manny swims in a hotel's outdoor pool and expects to hear (intuitively) salsa music to energize him. Instead, he intuitively hears cheering voices. He believes an unseen radio broadcasts the voices instead of his intuition.

2) Unexpected Intuitive Sense: You expect a specific intuitive sense to communicate intuitive messages to you, but another intuitive sense communicates. Edwinna asks her intuition, "Will I be able to save money for a summer vacation?" She expects to feel (intuitively) a comforting feeling for "yes" or a discomforting feeling for "no." Instead, she intuitively speaks, "Yes!"

3) Unexpected Condition: You expect to receive intuitive messages while you're relaxed or calm, not while you're active or tense. Saul's nerves flutter while chaperoning twenty teenagers on a scientific trip. He intuitively tastes warm chamomille tea but thinks he imagines its calming effect. He listens to his intuitive messages while lounging on his jumbo bean bag.

4) Unexpected Timetable: You expect instant intuitive answers, but your intuitive senses communicate them hours or days afterward, supporting your best interests. Rosa asks her intuition, "Why am I so unlovable?" Three days pass before she intuitively knows to love herself first, though other people adore her. She would have doubted the intuitive answer on the day she asked the question as a result of her reluctance to self-reflect.

Your intuitive messages arrive in infinite ways.

27. In what strange ways does intuition answer me?

The more you use your intuition, the more your awareness expands to recognize intuitive answers that seem strange but are divine. The answers startle or frighten you enough to ask, "Where did that come from?" Four divine ways include wondering, questioning, surrendering, and reflecting.

1) Wondering. You inwardly or outwardly begin a sentence with "I wonder …." For example, you wonder what your medical tests reveal. Wonder why your friends are late for dinner. Wonder how to pay your electric bill. Pay attention while wondering. You trigger your intuition to communicate answers.

SENSING THE CAUSE OF DEATH

> I watched an afternoon episode of a forensic TV show. A young girl had been murdered.
>
> "I wonder what happened to her," I inwardly stated, knowing the cause of her death would be revealed during the show.
>
> In my temporal lobes, I intuitively heard a man's firm voice reply, "Blunt force trauma."
>
> The unanticipated intuitive answer startled me. Three seconds later, the show's narrator announced the young girl had died due to blunt force trauma.

2) Questioning. You inwardly or outwardly begin a sentence with the word "why." For example, you ask, "Why am I fortunate? Why do certain people have to try harder than others do? Why did the charter bus driver flash the headlights?" Pay attention while questioning. You invoke your intuition to communicate answers.

LEARNING THE WAYS OF PSYCHOPATHS

"Why do I need to buy this book?" I asked my intuition, as I stood and scanned Dr. Robert D. Hare's book *Without Conscience, The Disturbing World of the Psychopaths Among Us.*

In my temporal lobes, I intuitively heard a forthright voice reply, "To learn about various people." I decided not to buy the book, though its contents joggled my interest. I returned the book to its shelf and drove home.

For three days, I intuitively felt a persistent urge in my chest until I drove to a local bookstore and bought it—one of the best books I've read. It helped me comprehend why certain people act self-centered and manipulate others or commit hideous crimes with no guilt or regret. It satisfied my yearning to understand the underlying causes of negative behavior. I told my intuition to alert me before I encounter psychopaths.

3) Surrendering. You surrender after doing your best, though results seem disappointing. In the intuitive flow, surrendering reclaims your inner peace; you allow whatever happens to transpire without interfering. It differs from giving up wherein hope is lost. Pay attention after surrendering. You prompt your intuition to communicate answers or ways to continue.

COMPUTER PROGRAMMING CHALLENGE

In 1992, I spent several nerve-wracking hours coding a computer program for a college test. The sly professor warned the class about the program's complexity. I believed I could code it, until I surrendered due to mental exhaustion. Lines of code intermingled; my eyes hurt.

I sat back in my chair in a computer lab and shook my head knowing I did my best. I intuitively felt inner peace shower my body. "Where did that come from?" I asked myself. In my temporal lobes, I intuitively heard my inner voice reply, "All is well."

During the next class, I found out no classmate had compiled and executed the program. The professor decided not to count it against our grades and showed us how to code it. Surrendering paved the way to continue.

4) Reflecting. You reflect on someone or something on purpose or "all at once." Pay attention while reflecting. You signal your intuition to communicate answers and sometimes use memory triggers. These contain past memories to guide and protect you in the present and future.

SHREDDER RIPS

I shredded personal documents at home. I intuitively saw a rolling inner vision show the memory of the day I leaned too near the shredder's opening. Rotating blades ripped my shirt's right tie. I cut it to match the length of my shirt's left tie.

Heeding my inner vision's memory trigger, I stepped back and flung both ties over my shoulders to prevent a repeat incident. Before I realized it, my shirt's right tie fell forward. Rotating blades ripped it. I cut it again to match my left tie's length. In hindsight, tucking the ties inside my shirt or changing shirts would have prevented another shredder rip.

How many ways does your intuition answer you?
Keep counting.

28. What happens when my intuition can't reach me?

If an intuitive sense can't reach you or grasp your attention, another intuitive sense steps in. Your intuitive senses independently or jointly communicate intuitive messages to you.

Oscar opens his barbershop. His busy mind fails to notice that he intuitively feels an uneasy feeling near his barber chair. He notices intuitively smelling a greasy scent signifying a defective hydraulic pump. Gigi folds laundry. She's unconscious of intuitively hearing a thought pop alerting her to a package delivery on her front doorstep. She's aware of intuitively seeing a flashing inner vision show the package delivery. Jericho's body aches. In bed, he misses intuitively tasting liquid pain-reducing medicine. He grasps intuitively singing songs about swallowing liquid pain-reducing medicine.

For any event, including a life-threatening incident, your intuitive senses communicate to you until you reach the point of no return—a critical juncture in which it's too late to act on an intuitive message, no matter the situation. Life plays out for better or worse.

Hillary falls asleep while driving to night school. She intuitively dreams her car smashes into an oak tree. Then she intuitively hears a police siren and wakes up. A mile later, she falls asleep again. On her arms, she intuitively feels a pulling sensation. In her mouth, she intuitively tastes hot ashes. She awakens and sips caffeinated black coffee. If she continues falling asleep, the same or other intuitive senses will communicate warnings. She'll arrive safely at school or crash into an oak tree.

Use your intuition every day and ask it to communicate loud-but-comfortable intuitive messages whether you're awake or asleep. Your awareness of incoming intuitive messages will improve.

Your intuitive senses warn you about many events
until your time to react runs out.

HIGHWAY LANE SWITCH

For more than fifteen years, my gift of intuitive feeling stopped alerting me to potential traffic accidents. I had ignored my gift while driving and once suffered a grim accident totaling my car. Instead, my gifts of intuitive seeing and knowing warned me of travel dangers.

One afternoon, I drove home from work and turned right toward a major intersection. In my chest, I intuitively felt a leftward pulling sensation signify to switch lanes at that intersection. Seeing no hazardous reason, I still moved into the left lane.

Within two minutes, a fender bender occurred in the right lane. The offender had driven her car ahead of my SUV before I switched lanes. My gifts of intuitive seeing and knowing failed to grasp my attention, but my gift of intuitive feeling succeeded and protected me.

29. How do my beliefs affect my intuition?

Your beliefs affect the use of your intuition in positive and negative ways. Believe you have intuition, trust it, and act on its guidance, and you reap twenty-one benefits (see Question 11). When you doubt, ignore, or fear your intuition, you step outside yourself and depend on other people for advice and security.

Have you intuitively known a doctor's diagnosis was incorrect, but you relied on his or her medical expertise? Intuitively heard angels speak, but you accepted a minister's religious skepticism? Intuitively spoken a humanitarian idea, but you allowed a friend to talk you out of it? If so, you relinquished your inner power to external authorities favoring their own beliefs and interests.

Remarkably, people's intuitive senses communicate intuitive messages to them every day despite their negative beliefs of being too:

- Old or young.
- Poor or rich.
- Analytical or emotional.
- Passive or aggressive.
- Energetic or lethargic.
- Distracted or focused.
- Injured or ill.
- Educated or untrained.
- Religious or secular.

Ask your intuition, "What are my intuition beliefs?" Sense the intuitive answers. If you discover negative beliefs, sense the point in time they started and why you hold on to them.

Shane asks himself, "What are my intuition beliefs?" He intuitively sees a rolling inner vision show him at age five. The vision replays a scene: his mother demonstrated how his intuition attracted sinister ghosts. At age forty, he still fears ghosts. His beliefs change the night he intuitively feels a strong feeling that indicates to check on his four-year-old son taking a bath. He listens to his intuition and saves his drowning son.

Replace negative beliefs about your intuition with positive ones. Your positive replacements flourish when you grasp the enormity of your intuition guiding and protecting you every day. Speak and live the following affirmation:

I now accept my intuition with love and gratitude.
I use it every day for my highest good.

Positive intuition beliefs reinforce your intuitive walk—a convinced stride overflowing with intuitive experiences.

30. Can my intuition help me change limiting beliefs?

Your intuition helps you change limiting beliefs with your willingness and actions. Prepare to make the changes you seek. Know that your intuition never forces you to say or do anything whether it whispers or shouts. Focus on any area of life, such as education, law and justice, or talents and gifts. Then state what you believe about it.

Patricia focuses on her career. She states, "I'm not brilliant enough be an airplane pilot."

What are your limiting beliefs? Do you believe you'll never have a loving relationship? Excellent health? Financial security? Use your intuition to uncover the point in time your limiting beliefs started and why you hold on to them. One or multiple intuitive senses communicate answers zooming to the cause of what keeps you stuck in a holding pattern.

Patricia meditates and asks her intuition, "When and why did my limiting belief occur?" She intuitively sees a rolling inner vision show the memory of her parents shouting, "You're a loser! You're not brilliant!" Their outburst occurred after she, eight years old, dropped a crystal punch bowl that shattered on their kitchen floor.

She intuitively hears an angelic voice whisper, "You cling to their limiting belief about you due to your fear of success. You're afraid to look into their eyes and proclaim, 'You're wrong. I am brilliant!' Instead, you live up to their low expectations casting light on their insecurities and failures. You disappoint no one but yourself."

Sensing the time period and underlying cause of your limiting beliefs—from childhood or adulthood programming—brings a shrewd understanding of why your life is the way it is and how long it's been happening. But no matter how many questions you ask your intuition and how much guidance it communicates, nothing changes until you replace your limiting beliefs with unlimited ones. It's like pulling up dead weeds in your heart and planting fresh roses there. Use your intuition along with meditation, journaling, and counseling, if needed, to live your biggest dreams.

Patricia willingly uproots her parents' limiting belief, which inhibited her for twenty-seven years. She intuitively sings, "Poisonous lie, be gone forever." Taking action, she studies for her pilot's license. Her new belief declares, "I am brilliant enough."

Your intuition uncovers limiting beliefs.
Rescue yourself from society's prisons.

---

31. Does intuition work with the Law of Attraction?

The Law of Attraction is a spiritual law allowing you to attract desired things (e.g., love, employment, money) in your life, aligned with your clear and unwavering thoughts, emotions, and actions. Believe you can have what you desire. Believe you deserve it. Be grateful and visualize your desires as existing manifestations in your life.

Your intuition is a spiritual gift communicating intuitive messages whether you support or sabotage your desires. Have you sensed the right actions to fulfill your desires even though those actions seemed illogical or unproductive? Trust your intuition to help you attract desired things and act on its guidance.

For example, you desire to own a two-story home in an affluent neighborhood. You intuitively feel a joyful feeling or rough sensation while visiting well-to-do areas of a city. Your joyful feeling alerts you to superb places to live. Your rough sensation alerts you to troubled spots to avoid.

If sabotaging thoughts or emotions rebound, your intuition communicates inspiration. You think your dream home is unaffordable, or you feel swamped with debt. Then you intuitively hear encouraging words "Believe you can afford. See yourself living in it."

If sabotaging actions arise, your intuition communicates a warning. You ponder blowing the down payment on a shopping spree, or you agonize about a bank loan rejection. Then you intuitively speak, "My dream home vanishes thanks to silly habits."

Your intuition also communicates intuitive messages when your desires will manifest later than anticipated. It's in your best interest to move at a slower pace. You intuitively feel an arresting feeling that indicates to wait and save extra money. Your inner guidance lessens your financial strain caused by unexpected medical bills.

The Law of Attraction and your intuition join forces
to facilitate you manifesting your heartfelt desires.

ATTRACTING A NEW JOB

I desired a new job. I stipulated my salary range, a short commute time, and a friendly work environment. In my temporal lobes, I intuitively heard my inner voice say, "Start preparing."

I prayed and updated my resume. Then I uploaded it to Internet job sites. I finished home and yard upkeep and rearranged dental appointments so I wouldn't interrupt my new job to carry out those activities.

In my bones, I intuitively felt certain I would obtain a job. I didn't fixate on particular companies, buildings, or vicinities—somewhere I had a desk, phone, and computer. Nothing deterred me, not the economic recession or job layoffs. Three weeks later, I completed a phone interview and received a job offer that same day. I attracted my desired job.

32. Which feelings and sensations belong to me?

If a feeling or sensation belongs to you, you know or sense the reason. For instance, you feel delighted before winning a church raffle, you feel heat while touching an electric blanket, or you feel sadness after an adored pet dies.

If a feeling or sensation belongs to someone else, you wonder why you feel unbalanced or disoriented until you find the cause. For example, you intuitively feel an itching sensation and then hear news about a co-worker's poison ivy rash. You intuitively feel a loving feeling and discover a nephew eloped with his girlfriend. You intuitively feel angry while driving in rush hour traffic and spot a driver filled with road rage.

OTHER PEOPLE'S DRAMAS

You suddenly or gradually absorb other people's feelings and sensations as though they're yours, regardless of where you are. Leading locations include homes, offices, churches, schools, theaters, restaurants, bars, and airports. We're all spiritually connected like drops of water in an ocean. Each drop of water carries the life happenings of other drops.

Grasp how you feel while reading books and newspapers, talking to relatives and strangers, and watching TV and Internet news. Do you emotionally connect with an individual or a group? Do you feel happy or miserable? Sympathetic or unforgiving? Friendly or hostile?

Are you uncertain that a feeling or sensation belongs to you? Ask your intuition one of the following questions:

- Why do I feel this way?
- Why don't I feel like myself?
- Why did my mood change?
- Why do I lose control of my emotions?
- Why am I thinking odd thoughts?

Sense the intuitive answer. Trust your intuition even with ridiculous and far-fetched responses. Validations come today or later.

Terrie sits in her art lounge and intuitively feels a sickening feeling. "Why do I feel this way?" she asks her intuition. She intuitively sees a paused inner vision show her ailing sister's lavender sweater that she wears. Terrie pulls off the sweater; her sickening feeling vanishes.

Hector loads groceries in his jeep's trunk. His mood changes from joy to depression. "Why did my mood change?" he asks his intuition. He intuitively hears an angelic voice reply, "You absorbed a butcher's health state while chatting with her in the meat department. Pray it away. Declare it's gone."

INTUITIVE FEELINGS AND SENSATIONS

The list of intuitive feelings and sensations is limitless. Intuitive feelings include calmness, certainty, disharmony, excitement, joy, and resistance. Intuitive sensations include coldness, dizziness, pounding, rockiness, stomach knots, and vibes. To know what each feeling and sensation means relative to your intuitive experiences, identify how you feel and where you feel it in your body. At the same time, sense who owns the feeling or sensation—you or someone else.

For example, you intuitively feel excitement in your heart and then receive unanticipated money. Intuitively feel stomach knots prior to your vehicle's engine breaking down. Intuitively feel a disharmonious feeling in your chest before encountering a rude restaurant host. Intuitively feel watery eyes and spot a child crying about a broken race car track. In the last two examples, the disharmonious feeling and watery eyes sensation respectively belong to the restaurant host and crying child.

Intuitive feelings and sensations can hold diverse meanings per intuitive experience. Sense the correct interpretations each time.

On Thursday, Penny spots a friend at a gym and intuitively feels pain in her knees. He admits to injuring his knees while rock climbing. On Friday, Penny sits beside a director at a company meeting. She intuitively feels pain in her knees. She absorbs the anguish the director feels for not standing and expressing his fiscal views.

PHYSICAL SIDE EFFECTS

I have clients who are stressed, exhausted, and overweight from constantly listening to or empathizing with other people's dramas. Some face-to-face, phone, email, and text messaging conversations serve toxic injections. Similar toxic injections happen while they watch TV, movie, and Internet dramas. These injections result in their energy drains, body aches, weight gain, and transferred illnesses.

I advise clients to, "Get rid of those real and fictional people living inside you. Eject their soap operas."

If toxic injections happen to you, pray, meditate, bathe, or exercise to cleanse them away. Use shielding techniques (see Question 44) to protect yourself at home and in the world each day. If you encounter trouble cleansing away other people's dramas, ask God or your angels to release them from your being. Feel the energetic relief within seconds or minutes.

Sense how many people live inside you.
Say goodbye to multiple existences and be yourself.

Pain Transference

I intuitively felt severe stomach cramps two hours after talking to a friend on the phone. I departed the art and craft store I shopped in, sped home, and swallowed two aspirins. I'd absorbed her physical pain as though it belonged to me.

Months later, I read about pain transference: mental, emotional, physical, and/or spiritual pain transmissions occurring between senders and receivers—people, animals, and objects.

"What else have I absorbed from others?" I asked my intuition. I intuitively saw an inner vision show how I intuitively felt a fourth grade friend's rejection the moment another friend refused to let her play with a doll during recess. Her rejection became mine. I fought for her right to play with the doll more than she fought.

My gift of intuitive seeing showed me other intuitive experiences in which I absorbed feelings and sensations of defenseless or timid people, injured animals, and discarded objects. I realized I've had empathy all my life.

Shielding techniques, prayers, affirmations, and deep breathing, help me block the world's pain and pleasures. What an energetic relief!

33. What does a pulsing feeling in my body mean?

First, rule out all medical and environmental causes. In the intuitive flow, a pulsing feeling is a rhythmic or throbbing movement in an area of your body or throughout your body. It falls under the gift of intuitive feeling.

You intuitively feel hot to cold pulses within you while sitting, standing, walking, running, dancing, or lying down. The pulses are subtle, intense, or somewhere in between and could synchronize with your heartbeats.

A pulsing feeling in your body means that you:

- Feel positive or negative energies in the world.
- Function at a higher spiritual frequency.
- Experience a body, mind, and spirit healing.
- Undergo the opening or activation of a spiritual gift.
- Sense pleasant or unpleasant news unfolds.
- Feel the presence of God, angels, or spirit guides.
- Sense evolving shifts of global consciousness.

While you intuitively feel a pulsing feeling, ask your intuition, "What does it mean for me?" Sense the intuitive answer.

In the intuitive flow, pulsing in Deidre's feet means a job promotion lands her way. Pulsing in Kenny's forehead means the activation of his gift of intuitive seeing. Pulsing in Robyn's lower back means a physical healing is in progress.

Intuitive pulses synchronize you to the beats of personal and universal spiritual happenings.

34. Why does my mood change as I enter buildings?

Your mood swiftly or gradually changes as you enter buildings and sense a single event or multiple events from the past, present, and future. Details hit you while walking through front, side, or back doors.

Have you entered a home and intuitively felt welcomed or unwelcomed by its occupants? Visited a hospital and intuitively felt valor or fear spew from roaming spirits undetected by your physical senses? Stepped inside a hotel and intuitively felt a comedy or tragedy would occur there?

Your mood changes fall under the gift of intuitive feeling. Identify your mood before and after you enter a building. For instance, your mood changes from happiness to sadness, confidence to insecurity, worry to comfort, or depression to exhilaration. Ask your intuition, "Why did my mood change?" Sense the intuitive answer.

Once you know the reason, release the mood-changing energy using affirmations, prayers, or other shielding techniques (see Question 44) that work for you. These techniques protect you against positive and negative energies affecting your wellbeing wherever you go. Or ask God or your angels to free the energies from your being. Feel the energetic relief in your body, mind, and spirit.

Examples: Mood Changes

Grumpy Bianca enters an arena filled with circus acts. She intuitively feels a joyful feeling and starts clapping for playful clowns. Her mood changes from grumpiness to joy.

Calm Felix walks through a side door of a furniture warehouse. He intuitively feels the residual tension of a week-old event: an irate repair technician threatened his supervisor with a loaded pistol. Felix's mood changes from calmness to tension.

Dejected Reese strolls into a health spa. She intuitively feels the jubilation of the spa owners due to their future financial success. Her mood changes from dejection to jubilation.

A building's life stories cause mood changes
for dear souls living the intuitive way.

HOSPITAL MOOD CHANGE

I drove to a hospital to visit a sick friend. I dreaded seeing her in a deteriorated condition. In my heart, I intuitively felt a surefire feeling that indicated she'd survive the illness doctors diagnosed.

Earlier that morning, I phoned to warn her, "Go to the emergency room. Your body is shutting down now." Death knocked at her front door.

"My boyfriend will drive me," she promised, shivering uncontrollably in bed.

During the afternoon, I intuitively felt a disturbing feeling in my spirit. A follow-up phone call revealed she still shivered in bed. Her boyfriend left for work without driving her to a hospital. Death waited by her nightstand. I called a mutual friend who left work and drove her to a hospital emergency room.

I entered the hospital's main entrance. My disturbing feeling changed to serenity. After a long walk and brief elevator ride, I located her room in the intensive care unit. Her face glowed despite her being dehydrated and near death. She received life-saving treatment for a surgery-related illness. Doctors released her four days later.

35. What is a first impression?

A first impression is the initial inkling—an intuitive feeling—you sense the first time you meet a person face-to-face or talk to him or her by electronic means (e.g., phone, email, webcam). It's also the initial inkling you sense concerning "a thing" the first time you encounter or handle it. A first impression grabs your attention by stating, "Here's the truth." It's instant like a burst of light filled with insight.

Have you met a stranger and sensed a nice or nasty personality? Received a job opportunity and sensed to accept it or turn it down?

Prepared to use a credit card and sensed security or identity theft? Your intuitive communication guided your next steps. Recall when your first impressions proved accurate.

You doubt first impressions when you think you're acting mean-spirited or judgmental. Or when first impressions disappoint you or shatter your beliefs about someone or something. Keep in mind that what you sense comes from within you—no reliance on physical appearances, body language, or direct conversations. Validations leave you saying, "I knew it."

Sense truth in an instant. Stay in the know.

First Impression: On-the-Job Training

"How do I truly know what I sense about my colleague is real?" a lecture participant asked me.

"Did it come true?" I asked without prodding her for details about her colleague.

"Yes," she sighed. "But I didn't want to judge her."

"You didn't judge her," I said. "You sensed who she is without anyone telling you."

36. What is the conscious and subconscious mind?

Your conscious is a part of your mind that's aware of your emotions, thoughts, beliefs, actions, and surroundings in the present moments. You make decisions with full, partial, or no knowledge of the true reasons contained in your subconscious mind. Your conscious mind detects many intuitive experiences in progress.

Sophia intuitively hears church bells ringing. The bells signal it's time to start her new food franchise. She's conscious of her intuitive experience as it happens, not in hindsight.

Your subconscious is another part of your mind functioning behind the scenes of your conscious mind. It regulates bodily functions, including breathing, blood circulation, and food digestion. It stores your emotions, thoughts, beliefs, actions, knowledge, and memories like an eternal computer database. Your subconscious mind detects and stores your conscious and unconscious intuitive experiences.

Clarence is unaware he intuitively feels a cautious feeling that indicates to steer clear of his bank at lunchtime. He enters the main entrance at 11:15 AM and bumps into three armed robbers. Unharmed, he later ponders the robbery and recalls his cautious feeling—the intuitive experience stored in his subconscious mind.

At each day's end, ask your intuition, "What intuitive experiences did I miss?" The question directs your subconscious mind to search its database and retrieve your intuitive experiences. They return to your conscious mind like unforgettable memories.

In addition, ask your intuition, "What intuitive experiences occurred during my lifetime?" The question also directs your subconscious mind to retrieve intuitive experiences stored in its database. You become conscious of them the same day and in ensuing weeks.

Your subconscious mind automatically retrieves your intuitive experiences to guide and protect you. It alerts you when you're on the verge of missing opportunities or repeating mistakes.

Nelly steps onto a four-foot ladder to hang a family portrait in her living room. She intuitively tastes joint pain. Her subconscious mind reminds her, "You ignored an intuitive warning the last time you stepped onto a ladder. It collapsed and you sprained your left ankle." This time she asks her husband to hold the ladder. She hangs the portrait and remains injury-free.

Your intuitive history is stored within your soul—
inerasable, retrievable, and valuable.

37. Can my intuition help me make the right decisions?

Your intuition helps you make the right decisions for any area of life, including career, education, finances, and transportation. Intuitive advisories communicate your finest choice or best course of action step-by-step or all together.

During your lifetime, you make planned and spontaneous decisions. You choose clothes and shoes to wear, beverages to drink, and businesses to patronize. You choose jobs, doctors, and relationships. Sometimes you have days to analyze options and potential outcomes; other times require quick responses. Do you base your decisions on facts, desires, beliefs, habits, or something else? Regardless, intuitive decisions save you time, money, and energy.

Has your intuition ever tapped you to confirm your choices are on track? Has your intuition nudged you to select differently than your habits or inclinations? Did you follow your inner guidance or stick to your recurring plan or impromptu action? What happened?

If you prefer, research facts and figures before making a decision. Given they can be invalid or manipulated, ask your intuition, "What's the right choice for me?" Sense the intuitive answer. You could receive innovative options or directions for which no precedence is established. Act on the inner guidance you receive.

For example, you ask your intuition, "Should I enroll in college now to obtain a degree?" You intuitively:

- See a vision show an open door (yes) or a closed door (no).
- Feel a leaning forward sensation (yes) or a leaning backward sensation (no).
- Hear direct words "School is in (yes)," or "School is out (no)."
- Know the colleges to contact (yes) or to contact none (no).
- Taste bubbly champagne (yes) or a flat soft drink (no).
- Smell a washed shirt (yes) or a grubby shirt (no).
- Speak, "Study hard (yes)," or "Veto homework (no)."
- Sing, "Fill out an application (yes)," or "Wait a year (no)."

When a decision is right for you, you intuitively feel a peaceful or reassuring feeling in your body. The feeling may oppose your analyses or wishes. The right decision incites you to do an uncharacteristic act, for example: Leave your comfort zone. Reorganize your priorities. Renounce die-hard traditions.

When a decision is wrong for you, you intuitively feel a resistant or tense feeling in your body. You might think you know best and other people encourage you to "go for it." But your intuition prompts you to change your strategy, for example: Select a judicious option. Call a former colleague. Delay your deals.

For each decision, ask your intuition additional questions: Why this choice? What's the perfect timing? What else do I need to know? Sense the intuitive answers. Act on the inner guidance you receive.

Examples: Intuitive Decision-Making

Intuitive Seeing: Yeremiah asks his intuition, "Should I remodel my family room?" He intuitively sees a flashing inner vision show an illuminated green traffic light signifying "yes." (An illuminated red traffic light signifies "no.")

Intuitive Feeling: Priscilla contemplates raising cats. In her ears, she intuitively feels a clogged sensation indicate the timing is wrong. (An unclogged sensation indicates the timing is right.)

Intuitive Hearing: DeAngelo contemplates asking his girlfriend to marry him. He intuitively hears his inner voice whisper, "I do not." (A whispering of "I do" means to proceed.)

Intuitive Knowing: Chaundra investigates small cities to relocate to during summer. She intuitively knows which cities ease her allergies. (She intuitively knows the cities detrimental to her health.)

Intuitive Tasting: Kirk searches for real estate to buy. He intuitively tastes the number, eight. For him, numbers from five to nine signify to buy it. (Numbers from zero to four signify to decline it.)

Intuitive Smelling: A cousin asks Regina to baby-sit his three children. She intuitively smells onions. For her, an onion scent means "no." (A peach scent means "yes.")

Intuitive Seeing: Donte desires an adventurous vacation. He intuitively speaks, "Rio de Janeiro." (Hong Kong tops his preferred list.)

Intuitive Singing: Yvette needs hip replacement surgery. She intuitively sings, "Sweet Thursday in September." (She wants the surgery performed in August.)

Let your intuition be your primary decision-maker.
Watch your life flow like a graceful river.

INTERSTATE EXIT AND RE-ENTRANCE

As I drove on Interstate 285 in Georgia, traffic slowed down. The frustrating disruption occurred beyond my physical eyesight. In my chest, I intuitively felt a pulling sensation indicate to exit the interstate. Unfamiliar with the area at the time, I exited and assumed I'd find an alternate route home.

I intuitively felt a second pulling sensation indicate to drive on an access road. A minute later, I re-entered the interstate past the traffic accident. My intuitive decision saved me two hours.

38. When will intuition guide me to change directions?

Your intuition guides you to change directions when it's in your best interest or for the best outcome. It leads you toward or away from someone or something.

Laverne's intuition taps her to watch a TV movie versus a theater movie to improve family relations. Wallace's intuition alerts him to turn left at a crossroads instead of right to avoid a water main break. Patti's intuition tugs her to sign a music agreement with a new company versus a well-known powerhouse to receive a fair deal. Jurrell's intuition stirs him to contact a distant veterinarian opposed to a local one to prevent negligence of his Beagle's jaw injury.

In sensing inner guidance to change directions, ask your intuition, "What's the purpose?" Sense the intuitive answer.

For example, you ask your intuition, "Why is it best to accept the second job presented to me instead of the first one I want more?" You intuitively see a rolling outer vision show a creative work environment for the second job. Intuitively feel excitement due to making new friends. Intuitively hear a rapid phrase: large annual bonuses. Intuitively know you sit in a sizeable cubicle free of micro-managers. Intuitively taste a prestigious position you value. Intuitively smell an engaging career path with travel opportunities. Intuitively speak, "No sexual harassment tolerated here." Intuitively sing, "I'll meet love on the third floor."

When changing directions is beneficial, for instance, you intuitively feel a convinced feeling or yummy sensation in your body. But when changing directions is unfavorable, for instance, you intuitively feel an out of sync feeling or a clammy sensation in your body. Listen to your intuition. Save time, money, and energy.

Your intuition advises you when to pivot your feet in a different direction.

CERAMIC TILES TO WALL BORDERS

I drove to a home improvement store to purchase ceramic tiles to line my bathtub. A store employee helped me select the items required to finish the job. I rushed to checkout and swerved left to prevent my shopping cart from hitting a sales associate.

I entered an aisle displaying wall borders. I intuitively saw a flashing inner vision show wall borders—not ceramic tiles—lining my bathtub. I grabbed two exquisite designs. A second flashing inner vision showed unused borders in my bathroom container. I bought them years ago to match my shower and window curtains. Changing directions, I re-shelved all the items in my shopping cart. I saved money, time, and energy installing old borders versus new tiles.

39. When will my intuition pass on new guidance?

Your intuition passes on new guidance whether you listen to or ignore its previous instructions. It acts like a tour guide communicating updates at each bus stop.

Shelly drives to a healing center and intuitively hears a cool voice say, "Take Exit 15." She listens to her intuition, though the exit leads to an untested route. Then she intuitively speaks, "This winding road ends at the healing center a mile ahead on the right." Her new inner guidance steers her to a convenient entrance.

Reggie intuitively knows to stay away from a house party because gunfire will erupt. He ignores his intuition and catches a ride there. Gunfire erupts at 1:20 AM. Then he intuitively feels a leaning forward sensation indicate to escape through a first floor window and run to safety. His new inner guidance, if he acts on it, protects him from suffering an injury or worse.

Have you sensed to deal with a distraught friend in a specific way and then sensed to handle him or her as normal later that day? Have you sensed to visit a store to buy a popular product and then sensed to drop by a warehouse to buy a rare product? Have you sensed to decrease your driving speed to avoid getting a speeding ticket and then sensed to decelerate more to miss hitting a crawling animal? Listen to your intuition for new guidance.

Intuitive updates bestow happier and safer outcomes.

NUMEROLOGY CLASS

In the 1990s, I enrolled in a numerology class held in Washington, D.C. In my bones, I intuitively felt a funny feeling that indicated I'd waste my time. My funny feeling stayed within me as I left work, parked my car, and boarded a metro train.

During the class, I became irritated. I learned nothing new and could have used the time for needed sleep. I blamed myself for ignoring my intuition and not the instructor teaching the class.

At the halfway point, new inner guidance surfaced. In my body, I intuitively felt a laid-back feeling that indicated to enjoy the class and friendly participants—make the most of it. I stayed until the class ended.

40. Is it normal to receive intuitive messages as I wake up at different times?

It's normal to receive intuitive messages as you wake up—night or day. Waking up is another altered state of consciousness. In this transitional state, you're receptive to intuitive messages with your eyelids open, closed, or reopening. You intuitively see, feel, hear, know, taste, smell, speak, or sing them.

As you wake up, lie still to grasp details. Movement could result in fractured or forgotten intuitive messages. Keep your intuitive journal and a pen or pencil by your bedside to capture your intuitive messages once you fully awaken. Or use a portable tape recorder or your cell phone's voice recorder.

Your intuition communicates while you're awake, asleep, and in between—altered states of consciousness.

Poetic Awakening

As I awakened one morning, in my temporal lobes, I intuitively heard an identifiable woman speak in a vigilant poetic form:

> *The world is a sorry place*
> *Gravy water*
> *I see a white light and in all its glory*
> *It can't stop me from going insane*
> *I know I'll get myself in trouble with the Lord*
> *Riding the gravy train*
> *Can a blind man see if he wants to?*
> *Can I do the right thing?*

I empathized with her troubles as though her war to live a virtuous life triggered my war. She rode the gravy train: a sultry money-driven affair. She questioned her willpower to make right choices; even spiritual enlightenment in the white light might not save her.

My poetic awakening exemplified how we're all spiritually connected like robust train tracks. We sense each other's pleasant and unpleasant situations whether we physically meet or not.

41. Can my intuition help me find inner peace?

Inner peace is a steady state of serenity that's always present for you to claim on your best and toughest days at home and in the world. This state is your "undisturbed self" or "untouchable self." Your inner peace is never lost; it dwells within you. No one and nothing can give you inner peace or deprive you of it, unless you allow it through your thoughts, emotions, and actions. Whether your problems persist or cease, your intuition guides you toward beneficial actions allowing you to experience inner peace surpassing human understanding.

For example, you intuitively see a rolling inner vision show you unchaining your feet from former indignities. Intuitively feel a let go feeling that indicates you choose to forgive others for baseless accusations. Intuitively hear your inner voice advise, "Stop listening to negative news and conversations." Intuitively know to sit on a river's edge to ease your anxieties. Intuitively taste healthy thoughts purging sickly thoughts. Intuitively smell hearty freedom after quitting unauthentic roles. Intuitively speak, "I accept what's uncontrollable in my life." Intuitively sing tranquil songs to silence pessimism.

Let your intuition guide your actions. Feel your inner peace rejuvenate your body, mind, and spirit.

Your intuition claims ever-present inner peace.

STORMY DRIVING

Driving through Nashville, Tennessee in 2009, I saw the pale sky darken during the afternoon. Monstrous clouds poured down rain. Inside turbulent winds, I gripped my steering wheel to keep my SUV from being blown off Interstate 40 and into a ditch.

Weather conditions echoed a tornado warning. I intuitively felt a peaceful feeling that indicated everything would be all right. Wind gusts pounded my SUV and other drivers' vehicles for nine minutes. My undisturbed self remained present. No tornado touched the ground and the fierce storm faded.

42. Why do I feel an urge to call or visit someone?

An intuitive urge falls under the gift of intuitive feeling. It is a forceful or persistent feeling toward someone or something. It feels like extreme hunger or a heavy burden rumbling inside you until you act on what you're guided to say or do. You intuitively feel an urge to call or visit a relative, friend, associate, or stranger because that person:

- Prepares to offer you a splendid opportunity.
- Plans to introduce you to an influential connection.
- Knows how to solve your problem.
- Holds important news to tell you.
- Thinks about you a lot.
- Needs assistance or cheering up.
- Is ill or injured and will pass away soon.

Call or visit him or her at once. You might ignore intuitive urges while you're busy, tired, sick, or lacking the desire to speak to that person, whatever your reason. It's your choice. Passing the point of no return—intuitive urge ceases—sorrow or regret grips your heart when you realize the missed opportunity to achieve a dream or the missed chance to speak to a dying loved one. Honor your intuitive urges and validate what happens.

Acting on intuitive urges satisfies spiritual hunger and lifts heavy burdens. Nothing else does it.

CHICAGO ON MY MIND

In my heart, I intuitively felt a persistent urge to call a dear friend living in Chicago, Illinois. My business and personal travels left me busy and tired. I finally called her but received no answer. Her answering machine had reached its capacity and no longer accepted messages. In my bones, I intuitively felt a disturbing feeling that indicated "something's wrong."

Weeks passed and I called her several times, but her phone kept hanging up. I left a message on her mother's answering machine. Two days later, her brother told me that she'd passed away from a third battle with cancer.

43. Why do I think about someone I last saw years ago?

That person's thoughts or actions contain energy broadcasting an intuitive signal like a radio station. Your intuitive senses receive the signal and cause you to think about him or her, though last seen by you years ago. Four types of intuitive signals are initiators, thinkers, travelers, and newsmakers.

1) Initiators: They plan to contact you via postal mail or email, by a phone call or visit, or by engaging a third party. You soon hear from them without your effort. Burl intuitively sees a paused inner vision show his ex-wife's heart-shaped gold necklace. She calls him within four days.

2) Thinkers: They frequently think of you and wish you'd contact them. They're unable or reluctant to contact you due to a lost phone number, a health crisis, a financial dilemma, or past remorse. If you decide to initiate the communication, they confirm, "I was thinking about you," or "You've been on my mind." Nadia intuitively feels shallow breathing that reminds her of an asthmatic college classmate. She obtains his email address and sends him a message. He replies, "I thought about you and our to-the-max crew. I'm recovering from a motorcycle accident."

3) Travelers: You bump into them in an unexpected place, such as a hotel, an airport, or a café. Orlando intuitively tastes double fudge brownies his former piano teacher baked for her top students. Three weeks pass. She yells his name at an outdoor music festival. He turns around and hugs her.

4) Newsmakers: Your ears perk up to hear pleasant or unpleasant news relating to them. The news comes "out of the blue." Theodora intuitively smells the cologne of a past employee. Hours later, she watches a TV news reporter praise him for saving two children from a masked kidnapper.

PREPARE FOR INITIATORS AND TRAVELERS

If you think about someone you last saw many years ago and have no desire to restore contact with him or her, consider what to say and do before hearing from the initiator or bumping into the traveler. This creates a satisfying outcome for yourself.

Will you stop and chitchat? Make plans to stay in touch? Express feelings you feared saying back then? Yell "hello" and "goodbye" in one exhale? Serve the cold-shoulder treatment? It's your decision.

You receive intuitive signals notifying you of
who thinks about you and who heads your way.

A GEORGIA REUNION

One afternoon, I intuitively saw a rolling inner vision show the blank face of a former Army roommate. I last saw her seventeen years ago during leadership training at Fort Gordon, Georgia. I wondered what happened to her and then set aside my inner vision.

A week later, I attended a book club conference held at a hotel in Atlanta, Georgia. I set up my vendor's table and heard a woman ask, "Do you remember me?"

I turned around and saw my former roommate. We hugged and talked. Her actions, flying from Virginia to Georgia to attend the conference, broadcasted an intuitive signal—traveler. My gift of intuitive seeing received her signal and communicated an inner vision, before I bumped into her in an unexpected place.

44. Why do things boost or drain my energy?

Everything is composed of energy, a living force communicated in vibrations or waves at various frequencies. Your body's energy field picks up positive and negative energies transmitted by people, places, and objects. The energetic transmissions pass through you like unruly winds or stick to you like adhesive tape. The transmissions cause your energy level to suddenly or gradually boost or drain.

Energy boosts and drains fall under the gift of intuitive feeling and affect you physically, mentally, emotionally, and/or spiritually. An energy boost is a force amplifying your capacity to be active. You feel excited, lively, or invigorated. An energy drain is a force depleting your capacity to be active. You feel weakened, tired, or irritated. Energy boosts are as off balancing as energy drains. They cause you to function above your normal energy level, making it a challenge to feel grounded.

People boost or drain your energy, depending on what goes on with them. Healthy, comical, and optimistic people boost you. Sick, pessimistic, and violent people drain you.

Rita's job woes increase. Her comical sister invigorates her with ironic humor; a sick brother weakens her with doomsday paranoia.

Places boost or drain your energy, depending on what transpires there. Exhilarating, magical, and peaceful places boost you. Dull, dilapidated, and noisy places drain you.

The Davidson family visits a magical amusement park. They feel excitement while riding a riveting rollercoaster but feel irritated while driving through a noisy city district.

Objects boost or drain your energy, depending on what occurs with them. Practical, functioning, and beautiful objects boost you. Worthless, broken, and dangerous objects drain you.

Arthur ventures on a solo photography expedition. An iridescent sunrise enlivens him; a broken jeep axle exhausts him.

ENERGY IMPACTS

Your intuition informs you when a person, place, or object affects your energy level. Have you intuitively felt stomach knots indicate to avoid a relative or friend on a certain morning? Have you intuitively known to make up a personal excuse to leave a corporate function? Have you intuitively tasted a corrosive flavor signifying to avoid eating a particular dessert? These and similar intuitive experiences protect you from energy boosts and drains.

Say goodbye to the person or thing constantly boosting or draining your energy. If you feel obligated to stay around him or her (e.g., spouse, parent, child), feel compelled to travel to a place (e.g., work, hospital, church), or feel forced to keep an object (e.g., picture, heirloom, vehicle), protect your energy field using shielding techniques.

SHIELDING TECHNIQUES

Shielding techniques are spiritual measures you perform to protect yourself from positive and negative energies transmitted by people, places, and objects. These techniques block energetic transmissions from affecting you wherever you are. Suggested techniques include:

- Call on God or your guardian angels to shield you.
- Ask your maternal and paternal ancestors to guard you.
- Visualize a white light, metal fence, or brick wall encircles you.
- Feel your body wearing a spiritual uniform, veil, or armor.
- Recite a protection prayer, affirmation, or hymn.

- Wear a blessed cross, crystal, or amulet.
- Sprinkle holy water or burn incense in your physical spaces.
- Create a protection mandala, collage, or jewelry.

Energetic transmissions affect you when you neglect to use shielding techniques or as techniques weaken over time. How do you know when you're affected? For instance, your mood changes from contentment to dejection. Your body temperature changes from warm to cold. Your energy level changes from lively to weary. Your wellbeing changes from healthy to ill. To cleanse away energetic transmissions you absorb in your home and in the world, go on nature walks, enjoy refreshing showers, or apply meditative willpower.

Perform shielding and cleansing techniques each day or week. Reinforce or change your techniques when you sense your spiritual protection decreases in effectiveness.

Your intuition and a spiritual protection plan
safeguard you against energy boosts and drains.

SHOPPING MALL DRAIN

In the 1990s, I arrived home exhausted after shopping in a mall for three hours. My energy had plummeted. I crashed on my living room's sofa until I recovered.

I read Dr. Elaine Aron's book *The Highly Sensitive Person* and Marcy Calhoun's book *Are You Really Too Sensitive?* I discovered I was a walking store-to-store sponge and absorbed the positive and negative energies of mall vendors, employees, and patrons. Crowds overwhelmed me. My revelation led me to use shielding techniques to protect me everywhere I traveled.

45. How can I know to be in the right place at the right time when opportunities knock?

At the beginning of each day, tell your intuition, "Let me know when opportunities knock." This statement sets your intent to receive intuitive alerts for you to be in the right place at the right time. Prepare to perform the necessary actions to maximize the opportunities.

Detach from analyzing "how" opportunities arise; the possibilities are endless. Let no opinions, doubts, or fears deter you. Opportunities happen whether you spot or create them. Notice what your intuitive senses guide you to do. For example:

- *Remain where you are.* You intuitively feel a stuck feeling that indicates to stay at your present location for a few more minutes. You see a former employer who hands you a residual check.

- *Go to a specific place at a specific time.* You intuitively see a rolling outer vision show you arriving at a town hall meeting at 6:00 PM, though you made no plans to attend it. Curious, you drive to the meeting and resolve a community issue.

- *Go to a particular location enroute to another place.* You intuitively know to stop at a convenience store on your way to a top bakery. You purchase a winning lottery ticket at that store.

- *Talk to a certain person at a certain time.* You intuitively hear the name of a friend to call at noon. He provides free tickets to an interior design show you wish to attend.

- *Listen to people's suggestions.* A friend suggests sipping a latte at a bookstore. You intuitively speak, "What a great find." You locate a rare book you hunted for months.

- *Do an uncharacteristic or impulsive act.* You intuitively sing a folk song in a fast food restaurant. You receive a chance to guest star on a local TV show.

- *Watch or listen to a radio, TV, or Internet program.* You intuitively smell an alluring scent signifying to watch a webinar. The instructor's tips lead you to develop a profitable children's game.

Sensing opportunities increases your life's breaks.

---

46. Can my intuition help me with my business?

Your intuition helps you manage every aspect of your new or continuing business. It communicates intuitive messages for you to sense the right goals and objectives, products and services, locations and layouts, financing and marketing strategies, and business partners and employees. Research business requirements (e.g., licenses, accounts, taxes) governed by local, state, and federal laws and regulations.

Whatever phase (e.g., planning, operation, expansion) your business operates in, pause and ask your intuition, "What's the right decision for <name the aspect>?" Sense the intuitive answers. Act on the inner guidance you receive.

Start by asking your intuition, "Have I instituted a clear vision for my business?" Sense a "yes" or "no" answer.

For example, you intuitively see a paused outer vision show a sunny or smoggy sky. Intuitively feel a light or heavy sensation. Intuitively hear one word "concur" or "disagree." Intuitively know your business vision is structured or vague. Intuitively taste a ripe apple or moldy pear. Intuitively smell vibrancy or boredom. Intuitively speak, "It's clear-cut," or "It's complicated." Intuitively sing, "I see clearly now," or "I feel upside down."

If your vision is unclear, ask your intuition, "How do I write an effective vision statement for my new (or continuing) business?"

For example, you intuitively dream a college professor instructs you to shorten your vision statement. Intuitively feel a fiery sensation indicate to add passion to it. Intuitively hear the command: write it, believe it, achieve it. Intuitively know to make it inspiring. Intuitively taste a twist of comedy. Intuitively smell where to research examples.

Intuitively speak, "Stretch all your accomplishments." Intuitively sing, "I'll add big dreams to it."

If you're still unsure, tell your intuition, "Help me write an effective vision statement." Allow the words to burst into your awareness without judgment or rejection. Examine the results.

Ask your intuition "yes and no" and detailed questions for other business aspects:

- What's an excellent name for my business?
- What's the right direction for my mission?
- Who is my target audience?
- What's the top location and why?
- Is this individual (or company) beneficial to my business?
- What products and services do I include or remove?
- What are the best financing strategies for my business?
- What are the best marketing strategies for my business?
- How can I win clients like nobody else?
- How do I improve my profits?

Studying existing business data, techniques, and statistics is advantageous for you. Reading business management books and articles is useful. But also trust your intuition to sense what's suitable for your business. Use your intuitive journal to record, track, and validate your intuitive experiences involving business affairs. If your intuition guides you to blaze revolutionary paths, then go for it.

Intuitive decision-making fuels business success.

47. How can I sense when people lie to me?

Sense what your intuition communicates about what's said and unsaid during in-person, phone, Internet, email, and text messaging conversations. Your intuitive senses identify which part, if not all, of a conversation is an unintentional or a deliberate lie. You discern misleading words. Read between the lines. Decode silence.

For example, during and after conversations, you intuitively see a rolling inner vision show the talker's nose grow like Pinocchio's nose. Intuitively feel an empty stomach sensation indicate omitted details. Intuitively hear spotty speech. Intuitively know he or she isn't giving it to you straight. Intuitively taste synthetic explanations. Intuitively smell fictional stories. Intuitively speak, "He's two-faced." Intuitively sing, "I lift bales with her tales."

Worry not about acting judgmental or faultfinding. Be at ease regarding electronic technologies that provide no face-to-face contact, thus blocking your ability to observe people's facial or body language and detect their lies. Your intuition never relies on physical closeness or cameras, anyway.

People choose how to maneuver through life. Unintentional lying is due to unawareness or forgetfulness. People's motivations for deliberate lying range from a desire for privacy to conformity to deception to self-preservation. Regardless, your intuition clues you to lies, giving you time to decide what to say and do.

Examples: Sensing Lies

Rod intuitively feels a disturbing feeling that indicates his employer lies while promising no job layoffs. He updates his resume. Layoffs occur within six weeks.

Marcie intuitively knows her fifteen-year-old daughter lies about her fundraising location. A GPS tracking device locates the teenager seven miles past charity booths.

Brooke's neighbor vows to fence his pit bulls. She intuitively tastes his biting lie. A day later, she spots his fence's chomped holes.

Your intuition is a foolproof lie detector.

A NEWCOMER'S WELCOME

I attended a newcomer's meeting held at a downtown library in Atlanta, Georgia. One of the group's longtime members acted as though she knew important connections and could assist newcomers with everything they needed. I intuitively tasted her bitter phoniness.

Later that afternoon, I stopped by the membership table and questioned her book publishing connections. Her eyes lowered and she backed off her earlier claims.

48. Can people use their intuition to manipulate me?

People can use their intuition to manipulate you but only if you let them. Manipulators sense potent words to speak to charm you, sensitive buttons to push to strengthen your guilt, tender heartstrings to pull to gain your favor, and silent treatments to apply to capture your cooperation. They also sense the ideal time and place—planned or on impulse—to execute their schemes.

Know when your intuition warns you about first-time or continuing manipulation from anyone—adult or child. For example, you intuitively dream you watch flattering tricks. Intuitively feel a pulling sensation toward an unsettling direction. Intuitively hear a distress siren close to you. Intuitively know a conniving force contacts you. Intuitively taste a distorted situation. Intuitively smell an oppressive power play. Intuitively speak, "Reverse psychology in effect." Intuitively sing a song spotlighting a controlling person.

Once your intuition communicates intuitive messages about manipulators, sense your counterattack: ignore them, reverse positions in the situation, stop your cooperation, or leave the scene. Intuitive strategies uphold your inner power against manipulation.

Your intuition identifies and counteracts manipulators.

Manipulative Husband

A friend told me how her husband manipulated her to pay their gas bill. He pretended to forget their fifty-fifty agreement—selective memory—though she explained it to him several times. Legally separated, he hounded her via phone calls and emails.

"Why did you pay the full balance?" I asked.

"He got on my nerves," she replied. "I just wanted him to stop."

He intuitively knew how to wear her down and save his money. I sensed he specialized in manipulation long before they met.

She lived according to her ethics and had difficulty understanding why some people exploited others.

"It's about what they want," I stressed. "They don't care about your feelings or care to do the right thing."

I emailed her links to Internet articles describing manipulators and their usual tactics. But I intuitively knew seasons would pass before she "got it."

49. How do I sense people as they are and not as they seem?

To sense people as they truly are, detach from what your physical senses record about them. Detach from what they say about themselves and what others tell you. Drop those details on a back burner. Then release the perception that people are born good, are good-hearted, or are saints traveling on earth. For some, goodness or saintliness makes well-timed guest appearances. Your detachment from prior knowledge frees up space for unfiltered truth to emerge.

I hear clients say, "She seems nice," or "He seems intelligent," or "Their relationship seems terrific." Seem is a word smoke screening your physical senses. Some people wear disguises and alter habits to fool you and others. Sense how much you believe the word "seem" is true while you say it. Rate your "gut-feeling" scale from 1 (no belief) to 2 (so-so belief) to 3 (total belief).

For a known or an unknown person, ask your intuition, "Who is he now?" Or "Who is she now?" Sense the intuitive answer.

For example, you meet a talkative stranger who seems obliging, but you intuitively feel a red flag feeling that indicates he's lazy. You speak to an older friend who seems to understand an awkward incident, but you intuitively hear your inner voice say, "She's unsympathetic." You visit a cousin who seems to face trouble everywhere he travels, but you intuitively know he's a peacemaker. You work with a colleague who seems unreliable, but you intuitively speak, "She'll beat her deadlines."

People sense pleasant and unpleasant details about relatives and friends they've known for years and strangers they've just met. They wrestle with feeling mistaken, insensitive, or judgmental concerning the unpleasantries. What "seems to be" blankets the truth but only to those doubting or ignoring their intuition. If this happens to you, consider two perspectives:

1) Who they are now evicted who they were in their younger days. People change in marvelous, typical, and despicable ways.

2) Who they live as now is who they've always been. In the past, they concealed kindhearted or malicious personality traits.

Your intuition informs you who people truly are.
Now you know what to expect and do.

FRIENDLY CHURCH MEMBER

"I'm interested in this man at my church," a client said. "Is he interested in me?"

I intuitively saw a rolling inner vision show his joy in talking to her but no loving feeling.

"He enjoys your discussions," I replied, "but he isn't looking for a serious relationship."

"He seems like he wants us to get together," she said. Disappointment lined her face.

"I don't see that happening," I said. "He also enjoys talking to another woman at your church."

She desired his love and silently doubted my intuitive message. A subsequent rolling inner vision showed his friendly, non-romantic interest, even without the other woman's presence.

"Ask him how he feels about you," I advised, knowing his response would erase her doubt.

50. How do I sense situations as they are and not as they seem?

To sense situations as they truly are, detach from what your physical senses record about them. Detach from the views of other people, including family, friends, associates, and the news media. Place those details on a closet shelf. Then release the notion that situations follow fixed patterns or preset destinies. Situations can change courses faster than jet aircraft. Your detachment from prior knowledge frees up space for unfiltered truth to emerge.

I hear clients say, "This situation seems hopeless," or "My circumstances seem uncontrollable," or "Nothing seems to change." Seem is a word smoke screening your physical senses as situations shift for better or worse. Sense how much you believe the word "seem" is true while you say it. Rate your "gut-feeling" scale from 1 (no belief) to 2 (so-so belief) to 3 (total belief).

For any situation, ask your intuition, "What truly goes on now?" Expect anything. Sense the intuitive answer.

For example, you hear office talk that two co-workers contracted measles, but you intuitively hear the word "shingles." You're involved in a traffic mishap appearing to be a teenage driver's fault, but you intuitively know an older driver sped through a red traffic light. You believe your family will forget your birthday, but you intuitively taste your favorite strawberry cake.

With practice, sensing the "truth" of different situations becomes easier. You discard the "seems" and live in the intuitive flow.

Your intuition informs you how situations truly are.
Now you know what to expect and do.

ELEVENTH-HOUR CONTRACT AGREEMENT

I received a contract cancellation from a corporation I worked for two months before its scheduled end date. I sat at my work desk and then asked my intuition, "What happens after next Friday?"

In my inner ear, I intuitively heard an angelic voice reply, "You'll get a new job."

"Where is it?" I asked.

"Atlanta," the angel replied.

"Who will it be with?" I asked and intuitively heard the name of the same corporation. "When will I start?"

"January," the angel replied—the present month.

My Q&A session with my intuition stopped; answers surprised me. My rehiring seemed improbable due to a lack of funding and job positions.

On the Thursday before my last workday, the hiring manager asked, "Have you found another position?"

"Not yet," I replied. "I'm still searching."

"Would you be willing to stay under a new contract?" he asked.

"Yes," I replied, appreciating my intuition's accuracy.

51. How do I sense constructive criticism?

Constructive criticism is a compassionate or respectful analysis or opinion spoken or written about you to improve your life. When you hear or see direct or indirect criticism pertaining to you, control your ego, feelings, and reactions. Ask your intuition, "How does his critique strengthen me?" Or "How does her critique help me shine my inner light?" Or "How does my self-criticism broaden me in life?" Sense the intuitive answers.

For example, you intuitively see a rolling inner vision show how constructive criticism propels your job performance. Intuitively feel a freeing feeling that indicates others admire your tenacity. Intuitively hear your inner voice say, "My minister's analysis inspires me to lose weight." Intuitively know a friend's opinion rings true for a personal relationship. Intuitively taste ripe criticism in business dealings. Intuitively smell its earning capacity for creative ideas. Intuitively speak, "My brother knows alcohol hinders my spiritual growth." Intuitively sing, "My parents challenge the mind games I play with myself."

In the intuitive flow, constructive criticism is non-judgmental and growth-oriented. The roaring and whispering voices of constructive criticism sound kind and harsh to grab your attention. At a conscious or subconscious level, you comprehend its value in your life.

Sense how constructive criticism rewards you
beyond your voiced and silent disbeliefs.

---

52. Can my intuition reveal my hidden strengths?

Your intuition reveals your hidden strengths during various life situations. People point out a power within you, and you intuitively feel certain they're correct. How many times have others complimented your management style—leader? Or praised you for changing static rules for honorable reasons—game changer? Do you make people laugh—comedian?

At other times, you reach inside yourself and intuitively feel your power rising to meet events. How often have you invented ways to appease chaos—peacemaker? Or gambled with winning results—risk taker? Do you step outside square boxes—trendsetter?

Relax and ask your intuition, "What hidden strengths do I possess?" Sense the intuitive answers.

For example, you intuitively dream the actor, Will Smith, and you pilot a super airplane—willpower. Intuitively feel bitter coldness for injustice—fair-minded. Intuitively hear audio recordings of you encouraging troubled youth—motivator. Intuitively know how to finish tasks—competence. Intuitively taste assorted ways to resolve dilemmas—creative problem-solver. Intuitively smell what lies on the horizon—futurist. Intuitively speak wisdom—teacher. Intuitively sing songs about walking in other people's shoes—empathy.

Let your intuition guide you to your hidden strengths. Use them in your personal and professional life.

Sense your hidden strengths. Live an empowered life.

A LESSON IN ACCEPTANCE

Stress ruled my first job layoff, though I had intuitively dreamed I stood in line at an unemployment office. My intuitive dream came to life a year later. My company's government contract and my telecommuting job ended.

In my inner ear, I intuitively heard my inner voice say, "It's time to get going." I learned to accept what's unchangeable—a hidden strength. Complaining and pointing fingers increased my worries and served no one. I intuitively felt a peaceful feeling in my spirit.

Thereafter, I intuitively dreamed I rode on a packed commuter bus. Its brakes failed. As the bus skidded off a cliff, the driver threw me into an ocean. I landed on a lifesaver's ring and then swam to a white sandy beach surrounded by flying doves. I made it to safety.

The dramatic dream forewarned me that another job ended before it started, but everything would end well. The hiring manager withdrew the job a week before our kickoff meeting in Washington, D.C. Two months later, I found a long-term job and made new friends.

Now when I hear news reports about job layoffs and firings, my peaceful feeling remains undisturbed. I acknowledge what's unchangeable and apply my faith and intuition to guide me to the next phase of my life.

53. Why do I doubt my intuition in bad relationships?

You doubt your intuition in bad relationships because it communicates intuitive messages interfering with the satisfaction of a desire. This desire reaches for love, power, money, companionship, excitement, attention, materialism, sex, or spirituality.

At a basic level, you sense whom to hang around and leave alone, what to allow and refuse, and where to mingle and bypass. You attempt to fulfill your overriding desire and hope for the best or crave a wild ride for as long as the relationship lasts. It's risky to see likeable or enticing qualities in someone and dismiss negative qualities. You insist, "He isn't that way," or "She'll change for me," or "He's met his match," or "She needs a good person like me." Your intuition communicates intuitive messages describing flawed human personalities so you'll make wiser choices.

In nowsight or hindsight, you sense warning signs. For example, you intuitively dream your other half sends text messages to a secret lover. Intuitively feel a distrustful feeling while meeting someone of interest. Intuitively hear a sermon "Avoid Marrying Dysfunction." Intuitively know to leave that shark in the ocean. Intuitively taste a spouse's deceptive jargon for working overtime. Intuitively smell a tainted scent regarding your date's claim of financial security. Intuitively speak, "A naughty individual steers into my town." Intuitively sing a song hyping a criminal companion.

I have clients who cling to bad relationships, old and new, due to a fear of abandonment or change. "At least I know my shady rascal," they rationalize. "There's no telling whose fiendish eye winks at you these days." Their intuition advises them to kick out their shady rascal. They hurt themselves in the end and know it all along.

You're free to choose your relationships. You're free to satisfy your desires. Intuitive wisdom says, "Listen to your inner guidance in advance to arrive at the right relationships for you." You save time, money, and energy. Sometimes you're guided to people you least expect because they support your desires and dreams.

Listen to your inner guidance to avoid bad relationships.

SENSING MANLY MOVES

I switch my intuition to automatic to sense details about men, after they approach me with a dating interest. No matter how handsome they look or how charming they act, I sense their life stories.

I intuitively see paused inner visions show their true marital status and the number of children they have. I intuitively taste their plush honesty or bankrupt dishonesty during conversations. In my chest, I intuitively feel harmony around good men and disharmony around the badly behaved.

Over the years, my intuition sharpened at work and in rush hour traffic, in classrooms and nightclubs, and at sports events and house parties. In the beginning, I knew nothing about inner guidance but dodged terrible relationships by paying attention to my intuitive expression: "Something told me to leave him alone."

54. How can I sense if my spouse is cheating on me?

Your intuition automatically or by request tells you that your spouse is cheating on you when it's true. Your physical senses provide clues. You see foreign hair strands on your spouse's clothing, overhear suspicious phone conversations, or smell unfamiliar fragrances on body areas. Your intuition forewarns you whether your spouse is awake or asleep and is present or absent.

Pay attention to intuitive warning signs. For example, you intuitively see a rolling inner vision show your spouse in a hotel room with a friend or stranger. Intuitively feel a rocky sensation during a kiss or hug. Intuitively hear disloyalty while you both talk on your cell phones. Intuitively know you're disrespected during overnight business trips. Intuitively taste a sneaky flavor while reading emails. Intuitively smell a deceitful scent lingering inside your spouse's vehicle. Intuitively speak, "Health club betrayal." Intuitively sing, "Your cheating heart can't hoodwink me."

It's best to delay accusing your spouse of cheating without physical solid proof or a confession. To sense it from your spouse's mouth, while standing or sitting face-to-face, ask him or her, "Are you faithful?" Sense the truth or a lie living in your spouse's reply. Reject outbursts of "You imagine silly things," or "You're crazy for thinking I'd cheat on you," or "You dishonor our wedding vows." Your intuition communicates the truth about marital affairs to help you make an informed decision to work on the marriage or call a divorce attorney.

Your intuition exposes married and unmarried cheaters.

Two Black Dresses

A friend intuitively dreamed her husband had an affair. Awake, she believed he was faithful.

"I dreamed I saw a large black dress and a small black dress lying on our bed in our second home," she said. "My husband stepped out of the shower. I asked him, 'What are these dresses doing here?' He remained silent and sadness coated his face. He knew I knew about the other woman."

She later validated his affair during divorce proceedings. The two dresses represented his mistress and her teenage daughter who had stayed in their second home while she was away.

55. How do I use my intuition to find a good personal relationship?

Write down your beliefs or standards for what constitutes a good personal relationship for you; it differs for each person. What does it look like? How does it feel? What conversations and activities transpire? What weaknesses and strengths endure difficult times? Review your list. Set your intent to use your intuition to guide you to your desired relationship.

Control desires and actions ignoring your inner guidance. These include craving ecstasy or wishing for somebody to come along and complete you. You're already born whole. Or you fear losing the seemingly best person to come into your life in a long time. Your intuition peers inside neatly wrapped human personalities set to commit or disintegrate. Walk away when sensing an individual is wrong for you, regardless of how attractive, charming, sociable, educated, or wealthy he or she is. Save yourself frustration and pain.

THREE RELATIONSHIP QUESTIONS

Before starting a new relationship or rekindling an old relationship, ask your intuition three questions:

1) Is this person right for me? Notice how you sense an attraction or repulsion, being turned on or off, warmness or iciness, or comfort or uneasiness.

2) What desires am I trying to fulfill with this person? Look within yourself and sense if it's love, attention, sex, or something else.

3) What's the outcome if I listen to (or ignore) my intuition? Sense what happens. A good relationship is your goal. A bad relationship results in wasted time, unfaithfulness, fraud, and/or violence.

Examples: Relationship Guidance

A cousin introduces Shania to an attractive co-worker at a law firm.

"Is he right for me?" she asks her intuition. She intuitively sings, "He's the guy for me."

"What desires am I trying to fulfill with him?" she asks and intuitively tastes coin-shaped chocolates signifying love and money.

"What's the outcome if I listen to my intuition?" she asks and intuitively sings, "He's my groom at the altar."

Chris meets a charming woman in a bookstore. They share a love for tennis and jazz music.

"Is she right for me?" he asks his intuition. He intuitively hears his inner voice reply, "No."

"What desires am I trying to fulfill with her?" he asks and intuitively hears his inner voice reply, "Sex and excitement."

"What's the outcome if I ignore my intuition?" he asks and intuitively smells a tyrant spoiling fun at social events.

> Good and bad relationships are sensed like
> lovely and bumpy rides before starting your vehicle.

Good Personal Relationships

Gwen intuitively dreamed her new boyfriend, Manfred, reached out his right hand and promised, "I'll never disrespect you." He kissed her hand and left her bedroom.

She awakened and intuitively knew that "he's a good man." She felt secure with him and intuitively heard her spirit state, "He'll become your husband." Married nine years, they have a three-year-old daughter.

Chelsea spotted Karl at a factory where they worked. He stopped by her machine and spoke to her before returning to his workstation. She intuitively felt certain he wanted to ask her on a date but ignored him.

She intuitively heard an angelic voice ask, "What are you waiting for? Talk to him." Thirty years later, they're still married.

56. Can my intuition help solve relationship problems?

Your intuition communicates guidance to help you solve relationship problems, but teamwork is vital. Intuition never forces anyone to do anything, even to save a dying relationship.

Relax and ask your intuition, "What's the true problem in my relationship with <person's name>?" Sense the intuitive answer with the understanding that the primary problem could differ from what you believe it is.

Jaclyn believes financial debt spoils her marriage. She relaxes and asks her intuition, "What's the true problem in my relationship with my husband, Gene?" She intuitively smells a sour pumpkin signifying his mother's behind-the-scenes meddling.

Once you know the true problem, ask your intuition, "How can I resolve <state the source>?" Sense the intuitive answer with the understanding that the solution could require irregular actions. Act on the inner guidance you receive.

Jaclyn asks her intuition, "How can I resolve my mother-in-law's meddling?" She intuitively hears inner advice: "Go for a casual walk with Gene. Spell out his mother's damaging martial impact." Jaclyn heeds her intuition. After three attempts, Gene silences his mother.

To solve relationship problems, you sense to carry out one or more of the following actions:

- Spend time discussing real issues.
- Find the middle ground mutually accepted.
- Go on a retreat and re-discover each other.
- Separate for a period to clear the air and start anew.
- Accept the person "as is" and decide to stay or move on.

Intuition solves relationship problems if both parties listen to their inner guidance and listen to each other.

---

57. Why do I intuitively hear music?

First, seek professional medical assistance if constant or unbearable music overwhelms you or interrupts your life; it could point out a health condition. Otherwise, you intuitively hear music because it's an additional way your intuition communicates intuitive messages to you. Music is universal, timeless, and impartial. Everything has a song, including people, places, things, and situations. Your intuition can use every song ever recorded to inform, comfort, inspire, entertain, and heal you. You intuitively hear songs in your temporal lobes, inner ear, heart, and "out in space."

In addition, you intuitively hear songs existing in outer space and in the spirit realm. Have you intuitively heard solar or nature chants? Ancestral or angelic hymns? Celestial bands or symphonies? Your intuition uses these songs to communicate intuitive messages to you in the same manner as recorded songs.

You intuitively hear music while falling asleep, during sleep states, while waking up, and throughout the day. Pay attention to the lyrics and musical arrangements. A song, in its entirety, may not apply to a past, present, or future situation, but its title, verse, chorus, bridge, or beat does apply. Song parts repeat for seconds and up to days, until you acknowledge them and sense their meanings for your life. What emotions, memories, or circumstances surface?

Have you intuitively heard a song and then turned on the TV and physically heard the same song play? Or caught a passerby whistling it? Or seen it written on a poster or billboard? Sense a song's meaning for your life even when its purpose is to make you smile.

Examples: Intuitively Hearing Music

Melvin visits his grandparents' home. In the basement, he intuitively hears the jazz song "Stompin' at the Savoy." He discovers his grandparents loved dancing to the song in their younger days.

Joy drives from Texas to Louisiana. She stops in the Big Easy and intuitively hears Fats Domino sing, "I'm walking to New Orleans." The song makes her smile.

A childhood friend gives Carlton a thank you gift. He intuitively hears the chorus of the song "That's What Friends Are For." Stevie Wonder, Gladys Knight, Dionne Warwick, and Elton John twice sing the chorus.

Alice waits at a hectic bus stop. She intuitively hears the title of Christina Aguilera's song "Beautiful." The angel-sent song changes her "I'm unattractive" belief.

Your intuition musically delivers intuitive messages.

SONGS VISIT MY WORLD

I intuitively hear music from several genres and eras. This intuitive experience occurred a long time before I realized its revelations.

I awakened at daybreak. In my inner ear, I intuitively heard cartoon characters sing an inspiring song "You Gotta Have Faith." The song told me to maintain faith in my ability to achieve my dreams.

On a different day, I sat at my work desk. I intuitively heard the song "Killing Me Softly." Roberta Flack and the Fugees sang it. Their renditions mixed without conflict despite dissimilar vocal and instrumental arrangements. I faced a spiritual transformation; a part of me softly died.

For two hours on a Tuesday, I intuitively heard the song "I'll Be Missing You" as recorded by Puff Daddy, Faith Evans, and 112. I intuitively knew that it meant an afterlife transition for an older relative. Ten days later, a sixty-plus cousin suddenly died in an Indiana hospital.

MUSICAL CONNECTIONS

I also realized I intuitively heard music while I contemplated, read, or wrote something. I contemplated driving to an animal ranch and photographing doves. In my inner ear, I intuitively heard the chorus of Prince's song "When Doves Cry."

I read an Internet news article about a grandmother winning multiple lottery prizes. In my temporal lobes, I intuitively heard Patti LaBelle sing her hit song "There's a Winner in You."

In my journal, I record an intuitive dream: I drove to meet a friend at a shopping mall at 10:00 PM. The mall had closed. As I recorded my dream, in my inner ear, I intuitively heard the title of Junior's song "Too Late."

58. How can I intuitively hear low intuitive sounds?

Relax and speak to your gift of intuitive hearing. Say, "Intuitive hearing, increase my inner audio to a louder but comfortable level." Expect it to happen. Next say, "Communicate an old intuitive message." Listen for an amplified sound.

Or visualize a tiny red "volume" knob is positioned inside your right or left physical ear. Visualize your right or left hand turning the knob clockwise to increase the volume to a louder but comfortable level. Say, "Intuitive hearing, communicate a new intuitive message." Listen for an amplified sound.

Prepare to hear numerous intuitive sounds, including music, conversations, and noises. For distracting or deafening sounds, tell your gift of intuitive hearing to lower the volume. Or visualize your hand turning the red knob counterclockwise to lower the volume.

Turn up the volume for faint intuitive messages.

---

59. How can I hear my phone ring before it rings?

You experience an auditory intuitive trigger—an intuitive message informing you of an incoming phone call from somebody unanticipated or somebody anticipated to call at a later time. That person's thought and act of dialing your landline or cell phone number contain telepathic energy signaling your gift of intuitive hearing. You intuitively hear your phone ring seconds or minutes before it electronically rings. Sometimes you sense who calls without glancing at Caller ID. Recall if you thought about or heard news about the caller prior to your phone ringing.

Does the auditory intuitive trigger sound like an old-fashioned or a modern ringtone? After changing your phone's ringtone, does the next auditory intuitive trigger change to match it?

Your intuition alerts you to incoming phone calls.

60. Can I use my intuition while I'm in poor health?

Use your intuition no matter how you feel. Your intuition is a spiritual gift—not a physical ability hindered by an injury, an illness, or a disease. As a spiritual/human being, part of your mission is to be healthy and heal physical, mental, emotional, and spiritual causes of poor health.

Anytime you feel unwell, ask your intuition questions: What is at the core of my ailment? How can I purge my pain? How can I heal faster? What can I do next time to prevent it? Sense the intuitive answers. Act on the inner guidance you receive.

Or say aloud or internally to yourself, "I am well." Claim it now. Listen as your intuition communicates intuitive messages to heal you.

You sense the right actions to restore your health whether you do it now, later, or never.

For example, you sense to visit a doctor, lie on your stomach, sit in the sunlight, recite a curative prayer, sing a healing hymn, avoid angry phone calls, or ingest herbal medicine. For grave situations, you sense to hurry and call 911 or contact a relative or friend to drive you to a hospital emergency room.

Examples: Intuitive Messages While Feeling Unwell

"I wish I felt like a million dollars," RJ says, watching college football on his dorm room's TV. He intuitively hears his godmother's inner voice advise, "Turn off that box now. Rest for one hour." RJ turns off his TV and naps for one hour. His headache ceases.

"How can I lower my blood pressure without taking medicine?" Inez asks her intuition. She intuitively knows to stop allowing people to mistreat her and then swearing about it.

"What place uplifts my spirit?" Amy, mildly depressed, asks her intuition. She intuitively sings, "Niagara Falls is a ball."

Your intuition communicates to you
whether you're in excellent or poor health.

SOFT DRINK REMEDY

I sat at my work desk and suffered stomach queasiness. *It's something I ate this morning*, I thought. *I wish it would go away.*

I intuitively saw a flashing inner vision show a cold soft drink. Initially, I resisted the caffeine buzz, but my stomach queasiness increased. I sprinted to the nearest vending machine and purchased the soft drink. I drank half of it; my queasiness vanished.

61. How do I speak truthful things while I'm angry?

Your intuition communicates despite your emotions. In the intuitive flow, your anger at someone or something allows truth to erupt from your mouth without prior proof or knowledge. Your thoughts hush as your gift of intuitive speaking reveals information.

> People ask, "How do you know that?" Or "Who told you?"
> You reply, "I don't know how I know." Or "No one told me."
> They distrust your mysterious exhumation of their buried secrets. A few people snub you but watch you like a surveillance camera.

In a negative manner, have you angrily wished a disease walloped someone and then discovered your wish came true? Lost your temper and hoped a neighbor's home burned, and then a gas explosion destroyed the home? Yelled at a police officer and swore you'd receive a fine for disorderly conduct, and then you had to pay it?

In a positive manner, have you blown your top concerning unfair treatment and uncovered an organization's corruption? Fumed about a career failure and used it to spur success? Argued with a friend and inspired her use of a rare talent?

In the intuitive flow, your angry words expose, predict, or cause things to happen. Be careful what you intuitively speak during fiery moments. Spoken words are irrevocable. Nothing is truly hidden, but certain truth has its right to privacy. Practice stopping angry eruptions. Pause and take a deep breath before intuitively speaking.

Other intuitive senses also communicate intuitive messages while you're angry. Pay attention to your visions, dreams, feelings, sensations, sounds, knowings, tastes, scents, and songs.

> Your intuition communicates intuitive messages during your irate highs and lows.

PROPHETIC OUTBURST

At one of my intuition development classes, a fifty-plus student stated her father died of brain cancer when she was twelve years old. At his graveside service, another man's disdainful comment about her father angered her beyond control.

"I hope you die from what my father did!" she yelled at him.

Twenty years later, the man died of brain cancer. Intuitively speaking, her angry words predicted how he'd eventually die.

62. Can I use my intuition while I'm stressed?

Use your intuition no matter your stress point or level. Your intuition is your spiritual gift—not a physical ability hindered by personal or professional stress factors that cause anxiety, irritability, restlessness, memory lapses, breathing difficulties, and rapid heartbeats.

Jenna feels uptight driving her three children to after school activities. She drops off her ten-year-old daughter at cheerleading practice. She intuitively sees a flashing outer vision show vulgar boys taunting cheerleaders. She waits for the boys to show up and then threatens to call police. The boys vacate the area.

Jonas and Veronica worry their middle son will overdose on drugs. They intuitively know to contact an eccentric drug interventionist to save his life.

Neil mulls over his twenty-year high school reunion; his heartbeats accelerate. "How can I lighten my nerves?" he asks his intuition. He intuitively speaks, "Go to comedy clubs." Less uptight, he attends his reunion and enjoys socializing with former classmates.

Your intuition guides you during calm and tense times.

GROCERY STORE CHECKOUT LINES

I left work feeling overstressed from afternoon events. I drove to a grocery store to buy a few items. In my inner ear, I intuitively heard a gentle voice advise, "Go to the second checkout line."

The first checkout line moved forward at an equal pace. I chose to test my intuition by defying its obvious guidance. I set my items on the conveyor belt.

In the first line, a customer started quarrelling with a cashier. She pointed out a product's incorrect price and demanded to receive it free. I waited three minutes for the cashier's price check while the second line continued moving forward.

If I had heeded my intuition, I would have exited the grocery store ten minutes earlier than I did. Still, I left the store knowing my intuition communicates whether I'm stressed or relaxed.

63. Can my intuition help me reduce stress?

Your intuition guides your actions to reduce your stress level that, if continuously elevated, leads to health problems. Your ego and other people pile on guilt and insults when you stop multitasking, facilitating, or volunteering. "Rest when you die," they say. Let them admire their time-crunched or people pleasing lifestyles.

Have you started home repairs and intuitively felt a red flag feeling that indicated to pay a professional to complete them? Ran routine errands and intuitively knew to switch a few to do later in the week? Managed a family calamity and intuitively heard your inner voice say, "You did all you can do"? Rushed to beat a work deadline and intuitively spoke, "I must pace myself"? Did you listen to or ignore your intuition for those and other situations?

During rising pressures, frantic moments, and restless silence, your intuition communicates stress-reducing messages:

- Pray for peace.
- Stand and stretch.
- Go for a walk.
- Talk to a supportive friend.
- Sleep extra hours.
- Avoid confrontational topics.
- Bypass TV news channels.
- Watch a comedy movie.
- Listen to soothing music.
- Enjoy a scenic train ride.
- Speak up for yourself.
- Learn to say, "No."
- End abusive relationships.

If you miss automatic intuitive messages, ask your intuition, "How can I reduce my stress?" Sense the intuitive answers. Act on the inner guidance you receive.

Listen to your intuition for stress management.
Embrace moderation and balance.

ON-THE-JOB STRESS

"Take a few days off work," I counseled a friend. "Your stress level is too high." I read her emails and intuitively felt her body's pain heave each word. I prayed to shield myself from her pain.

She dismissed my intuitive message and continued to clock in at her negative work environment with a bullying manager and intimidated co-workers. The next day, I received a frantic email.

"I passed out while I sat in my chair!" she exclaimed. "Everything went black. It scared me."

"Call in sick," I said. "Get away from negativity floating in the air."

She still ignored me. A few days later, she phoned me and said, "I'm at home. At work, my body started shutting down. It felt as if I was having a heart attack. Paramedics rushed me to a hospital. The doctor said what happened to me was stress-related. I'm surprised ... I'm in good shape."

"Stress can kill you no matter what shape you're in," I said. "Your body reached its breaking point. Change job positions or companies. The negativity mushrooming in your work environment will continue."

Two months later, she changed job positions and began working in a fun, positive setting.

64. Does intuition outperform emotional intelligence?

Emotional intelligence is the ability to identify, assess, understand, and manage your emotions and other people's emotions in public and private situations. It's a valuable skill enhancing your emotional and intellectual growth.

Both emotional intelligence and your intuition improve your social adeptness and effectiveness, but your intuition outperforms emotional intelligence. The identification, assessment, understanding, and management of emotions are contained in one to three intuitive messages per situation. You sense the emotions, the causes, and specific ways to respond.

Sabrina intuitively knows an uncle is downhearted when he arrives at her home. Opening the front door, she observes his composed facial expression, body language, and conversation. "Life is good," he says. But she intuitively knows about his concealed bankruptcy—his fear of generational financial failure. She intuitively knows the precise words to say to uplift him and impart a new perspective.

Augustine's co-worker is having a rough day. He intuitively tastes a stinging spat that occurred between her and her husband on the previous night. A shopaholic, she maxed out their ten credit cards—her childhood-driven need to feel worthy. He intuitively hears his inner voice warn, "Joke with her, but stay out of her problems."

THE EMOTIONAL DEFENSE

Some people say, "I'm too emotional to use my intuition." Believe you're too emotional, and you doubt or ignore your intuition. Believe you receive intuitive messages no matter your emotional condition or emotional intelligence skills, and you unleash your intuition.

Your intuition communicates the truth despite the positive and negative emotions you experience each day. While feeling sad, disappointed, ashamed, or fearful, ask your intuition what to do. Sense the intuitive answer. Act on the inner guidance you receive. You could sense to meditate, talk to the person(s) sparking your emotions, write or draw how you feel, or finish a creative project. Notice how your emotions change.

> Your emotions toss you on rollercoaster rides.
> Your intuition rocks steady.

FIRED TO HIRED

The company's president emailed a new nondisclosure agreement for employees to sign within thirty days or risk being fired. Her power play's injustice angered me, and I refused to sign the one-sided agreement, though I needed a job. I planned to relocate from Northern Virginia to Georgia and buy a home, realizing it took weeks to find a decent job. My emotions swayed between anger and coolness, haste and caution, and panic and self-control. I still received intuitive messages.

In my spirit, I intuitively felt certain that everything would be all right—the "How?" escaped me. The company's president called me and questioned my decision to reject the nondisclosure agreement. I intuitively knew she probed for details to entrap me legally on the prior agreement I signed. I explained my reasons, remaining professional and calm, but I yearned to rebuke her in one extended exhale.

She fired three colleagues and me on a Friday. I went to work for a growing company—unexpected job—the following Monday. Two months later, I relocated and retained my job, telecommuting from my new home.

65. How does my intuition cue me to reinvent myself?

Intuitive advisories cue you when to reinvent yourself. You're guided to change one thing or several things about yourself and your life. Your intuition whispers, "It's time to grow … time to express yourself." Intuitive signs spring up like cone geysers. Leap in the spouting waters to transform your body … your mind … your spirit.

> "Why can't I stay like I am?" you ask, comfortable or contented with the way your life rolls.
> "Become who you came in this world to be," your intuition replies.

Depending on your spiritual mission, your intuition advises you to reinvent yourself once or many times during your lifetime. For example, you intuitively dream you move to another city to start a new life. Intuitively feel a stirring feeling that indicates to socialize in progressive circles. Intuitively hear Jennifer Holliday sing "I Am Changing." Intuitively know a revamped appearance screeches your name. Intuitively taste the tender love of jaunty relationships. Intuitively smell vibrant health habits. Intuitively speak, "I create a legacy using my talents and gifts." Intuitively sing, "Community service is my ultimate passion."

> "I'm afraid," you cry, fearing an altered identity, other people's reactions, and an unknown reality.
> "Be bold," your intuition advises. "Fear traps you in a decaying existence."

While wrestling with "reinventing" fears, ask your intuition questions: What are my next steps? How do I handle my fears? Who will I be? Sense the intuitive answers. Act on the inner guidance you receive. Your intuition guides your steady pace when you start sooner than the last moment. Things work in your favor in unique ways.

When you ignore your intuition's whispers to reinvent yourself, it shouts, "It's time to grow!" Your contentment and comfort descend into boredom and misery. Then comes an intense hunger unsatisfied by any physical effect: food, money, technology, shopping, gambling, work, smoking, drugs, and sex. You're yanked out of your easy chair by a life-altering event or series of events: job loss, business failure, financial debt, relationship breakup, and/or health crisis.

Your intuition announces to reinvent yourself
to be the "authentic" you.

---

66. How can I use my intuition to be more creative?

Recognize that you're naturally creative. Everyone possesses artistic abilities known or discovered via other pursuits.

Relax and say to your intuition, "Help me be more creative in my life." Pay attention to creative ideas popping in your mind or spirit "out of the blue." These ideas fly outside conventional concepts and apply to multiple areas of life.

Anytime is the right time for a creative moment; anyplace is sufficient. Your intuition communicates creative ideas while you perform common and uncommon activities. For instance, ideas pop in while you brush your teeth, mail your bills, perform jury duty, teach a class, talk to a stranger, and climb a mountain. Your intuition also communicates creative ideas while you imagine, wonder, meditate, pray, daydream, and sleep.

You sense the right resources to use. For example, you intuitively see a rolling inner vision show you designing ceramic home decor. Intuitively feel a pushing sensation indicate to write a witty, futuristic screenplay on your computer. Intuitively hear precise instructions for choreographing dance recitals. Intuitively know ten original songs to compose on a guitar. Intuitively taste familial desserts to bake with modified recipes. Intuitively smell paper products to recycle for use in art programs. Intuitively speak, "I'm a motivating public speaker." Intuitively sing, "Making baby toys is beautiful noise."

Creativity adds universal fire to any profession or industry, including art, science, law, technology, economics, and medicine. Have you observed a global condition and sensed a practical solution? Used a household product and sensed other purposes for it? Watched an action movie and sensed an enhanced ending? If so, these and other intuitive experiences let you know that you already use your intuition in creative ways.

> Sometimes it feels as if you make up stuff.
> Celebrate your intuition-driven creative ideas.

FAMOUS PEOPLE AND CREATIVE WORKS

Famous people used their intuition in creative ways. It's reported that Mary Shelley intuitively dreamed the plot for her timeless book *Frankenstein*. Madame C. J. Walker intuitively dreamed the ingredients to make a hair care product, solving hair problems for millions of women.

George Washington Carver relied on God to communicate scientific insights through his intuition. It led him to develop many agriculturally-based products still benefiting humanity. The idea for the Beatles' hit song "Let It Be" came to Paul McCartney after a comforting dream he had about his deceased mother, Mary.

67. How does my intuition put things in perspective?

Your intuition shifts your attention to put things in perspective. This shift causes you to sense an unveiled outlook, an altered reality, the big picture, or a higher spiritual dimension. It's like focusing on a basin of water, and then your intuition shifts your attention to an ocean and its genius. Your view is greater than 360 degrees; time and space are transcended. You become receptive to unconsidered or unknown information that already exists.

Unveiled Outlook. Jared is upset with a client for missing a therapy session. He intuitively sees a rolling inner vision show his client sitting in a hospital's intensive care unit and holding her sick mother's hand. She calls and validates his vision. Now he understands her reason for missing the therapy session.

Altered Reality. Teddy leaves his dentist's office an hour later than planned and vents about driving behind sluggish school buses. He intuitively knows to change his mindset and visualize brisk traffic. He enjoys his ten-minute ride home, not the fifty minutes he estimated.

Big Picture. Linda wonders why her weight loss effort is stagnant. Her sister follows the same diet program with success. Linda intuitively hears her inner poem's opening line: I pile on pounds to repel unwanted sexual advances. Her willpower and eating regime, combined with professional counseling, help her meet weight loss goals.

Higher Spiritual Dimension. Manning intuitively sees a paused outer vision show two balls of light shining near his family's portrait hanging over a fireplace. He believes they're sunspots until the lights shine at night. He intuitively sees his deceased parents' faces glisten inside the lights. They spiritually protect his family.

When your intuition puts things in perspective, more possibilities wave at you. Limitations vanish. Illusions evaporate. An intuitive perspective aids your navigation in the physical and spiritual realms.

An intuitive perspective grants you elevated views exceeding earthly perimeters.

RED RENTAL CAR

In 1999, I stopped by a car rental company at Atlanta, Georgia's International Airport. A nice rental agent lent me a big red car that looked like a giant tomato on four wheels. I despised it and requested a smaller car.

"No small cars are available," she smiled.

That night, I intuitively dreamed I returned to the car rental company. I received a hideous green car that sickened me. It changed from a small hatchback into a sedan. I thought, *I should have kept the car I originally rented.*

My intuitive dream put my situation in intuitive perspective—an unveiled outlook. I felt grateful for the car I had. I could have driven a hideous sedan.

68. Can I intuitively study for school?

Your intuition helps you study for various schools: high school, college, trade, business, on-the-job, and personal/spiritual development. Relax and pay attention to instructive intuitive messages you receive before, during, and after your study sessions. You sense the:

- Best times of day or night to study.
- Favorable indoor and outdoor spots to learn.
- Optimal times to take breaks.
- Easy ways to improve your recall ability.
- Erroneous or missing details in assignments and textbooks.

- Course content to highlight to write essays and speeches.
- Correct answers to planned and surprise exams.

Examples: Intuitive Studying

Intuitive Seeing: Chauncey intuitively sees a rolling inner vision show he learns faster sitting outdoors near a tree or shrub.

Intuitive Feeling: Jean intuitively feels a gut feeling that indicates to memorize accounting terms. Those terms are included on a surprise exam two days later.

Intuitive Hearing: Barkley intuitively hears a referee's whistle blow when considering the right materials to study to obtain his GED.

Intuitive Knowing: Ophelia studies for her driver's license exam. She intuitively knows the driver's handbook contains errors and contacts the publisher.

Intuitive Tasting: Jasper intuitively tastes warm air signifying to take a break, walk outdoors, and bask in the sunshine for ten minutes. He returns to finish his medical assignment and discovers his recall ability has improved.

Intuitive Smelling: Cicely intuitively smells morning dew signifying daybreak is the best time for her to study for a work certification.

Intuitive Speaking: Manu intuitively speaks, "I'll research this procedural outline." At a night class, his college professor instructs students to write an essay on the same outline.

Intuitive Singing: Kelly intuitively sings self-empowering songs to support her passing on-the-job tests.

Study the intuitive way and praise your achievements.

ADDITIONAL TECHNICAL BOOK TO STUDY

I studied for a five-hour Information Technology (IT) Security certification using technical books and Internet sites offering practice exams. The certification covered more than twenty years. In my chest, I intuitively felt a tugging feeling that indicated to study specific areas.

One afternoon, I intuitively felt a pushing feeling in my upper back. My intuitive feeling indicated to drive to a bookstore and buy another technical book to study. I resisted the extra expense and information overload until I decided to listen to my intuition. I bought the book and read it. It helped me pass the exam.

69. How do I sense when my computer will fail?

You sense an imminent computer failure, for example, when you intuitively see a rolling inner vision show a flashing red light. Intuitively feel a rushing sensation to wrap up your activities. Intuitively hear the word "crash." Intuitively know to save your work to a storage device. Intuitively taste an electrical error. Intuitively smell a frozen program. Intuitively speak, "Next, a blue screen." Intuitively sing a song imitating buzzing noises. Your intuition warns you about failures from the moment you switch on your computer until you switch it off.

Computer failures happen due to hardware malfunctions, software bugs, virus infections, hacker attacks, and power outages. It matters not that your computer is new or old with no earlier problems. Your level of technical expertise carries credibility, but a computer and its components and software are fallible and hackable.

Trust your intuition. Finish your activities. Save your work. A failure happens within seconds or minutes after you receive the "hurry" intuitive message. Prevent stress and lost time from having to restart activities or recreate work. Stop your hindsight's remorse: "I doubted my computer would crash, then it happened."

Quick intuitive actions minimize or eliminate disasters.

Lost Video Edits

I edited a video file on my home computer. I intuitively felt a rushing sensation indicate to save my work "right now." I doubted my intuition because the new video editing program worked fine that day, and I required only ten minutes to finish my project.

Within seconds, the program froze. Selecting options or saving completed work proved impossible. I had to kill the program and restart it and redo my lost edits.

70. How do I use my intuition to protect my finances?

The first step is to decide to use your intuition in your financial dealings, no matter your current circumstances and despite what financial experts advise. Each week or month, ask your intuition, "How do I protect my finances?" Sense the intuitive answers. Act on the inner guidance you receive to save or increase your money.

If something sounds too good to be true or is valid but unsuitable for you, trust your intuition's financial advisories and march away. Sense when generosity or greed yearns to override your inner guidance. Stay in the intuitive flow.

When the potential for financial loss exists, you receive intuitive alerts. For example, you intuitively dream a bogus check is written to you for services rendered. Intuitively feel tension in your body as a friend asks to borrow money without a signed repayment plan. Intuitively hear a parental voice counsel, "Stop investing in worthless real estate." Intuitively know to turn down a misleading home insurance policy. Intuitively taste a dry streak while gambling at a casino. Intuitively smell sour peas signifying higher county taxes to pay. Intuitively speak, "No multi-level marketing groups for me." Intuitively sing, "I file a lawsuit against my employer and drown in debt."

When the potential for financial gain exists, you receive intuitive alerts. For example, you intuitively see a paused inner vision show a secret inheritance to collect. Intuitively feel bliss in your heart while scanning a missing pet poster displaying a reward. Intuitively hear an announcement: invest in rising stock now. Intuitively know winning lottery numbers to play. Intuitively taste sweet success after entering a singing contest. Intuitively smell cold cash after spotting a valuable painting at a flea market. Intuitively speak, "I audition for an assured movie role." Intuitively sing, "I'm rich with creative ideas."

Recall an occasion when you ignored your intuition and lost your money. Then recall an occasion when you listened to your intuition and saved or increased your money. What intuitive alerts emerge in hindsight? Trust your intuition. Save yourself financial remorse.

Listen to your intuition's financial advisories for monetary savings and increases.

A TIME TO SAVE

A cousin asked to borrow $800 for his upcoming court case. In my stomach, I intuitively felt a sinking feeling that indicated unrecoverable cash, though we shared no history of money lending. I listened to his legal quandary and family troubles but made no plan to wire him a single dime.

A TIME TO INCREASE

In my bones, I intuitively felt a surefire feeling that indicated to sell stock valued at $62 a share. I'd purchased the stock at $18 a share. I also intuitively felt a blocked feeling that indicated the stock's value neared its peak. I sold the stock and enjoyed the profits. My intuitive feelings proved accurate.

71. How do I discover what I love to do?

Relax and ask your intuition, "What do I love to do?" Then ask your intuition, "How can I use what I love to do to make money, support myself, and help others?" Sense the intuitive answers. Act on the inner guidance you receive. Keep in mind that what you love to do could be multiple activities and your life purpose.

For example, you intuitively dream you play a musical instrument (musician, music instructor). Intuitively feel a confident feeling to act in movies (actor, stunt expert). Intuitively hear candy limericks (candy maker, candy shop owner). Intuitively know you battle for justice (lawyer, activist). Intuitively taste assorted cuisine (restaurant chef, food critic). Intuitively smell bouquets of flowers (florist, gardener). Intuitively speak, "I love stallions." A horse owner or trainer suits you. Intuitively sing, "Farm life is for me." A farmer or rancher tops your list.

LOVING CHILDHOOD MEMORIES

Your intuition unearths childhood memories using one or multiple intuitive senses. What you loved doing as a child, you love doing as an adult in a similar or modified way. Allow the memories to emerge into your awareness without dwelling on which ones unlock the door to your happiness and success.

For example, vivid memories surface and show you playing games (game inventor, game show contestant); participating in sports (professional athlete, athletic coach); fancying artwork (landscape painter, graphic designer); caring for animals (veterinarian, pet shop owner); admiring words (novelist, poet); or cracking crimes (forensic scientist, police officer). What do your memories reveal?

THRILLING SIGHTS AND SOUNDS

Your intuition communicates intuitive messages while you observe or hear about an individual or a group involved in an activity thrilling your soul. You imagine yourself involved in the same activity.

For example, you observe people climbing a mountain and intuitively feel goose bumps indicate you belong there (mountain climber, hike leader). You hear weather reports and intuitively know your role (meteorologist, storm chaser). You watch a comedy program and intuitively dream you make people laugh (comic, clown).

Use your intuition to sense what you love doing and do it. If you progress in stages, beginning is winning. If you give up lifelong habits, your new walk and talk rise above routines. When you say goodbye to naysayers, you're free of dead weight.

Your intuition reveals your greatest loves in life.

INSPIRATIONAL PHOTOGRAPHER

In October 2001, I hiked with a newcomers' group in Helen, Georgia. I used my 35mm camera to capture autumn's beauty. The first time I saw my photographs, I intuitively felt a stirring sensation in my spirit.

Using computer equipment and graphic design software, I created inspirational photographs. I mailed the first set to family and friends who loved receiving them as much as I loved creating them.

I intuitively saw rolling inner visions show me selling my photographs at art and craft festivals. I heeded my intuition and started a business. My customers' support and appreciation proved priceless and led me to create complementary products.

During childhood, I snapped pictures of many family members and friends for fun and memories. I recall the 110mm camera I used then and my movement to digital technology. Inspirational photography lolled outside my career plans until the day I saw my nature photographs.

72. How does my intuition improve time management?

Intuitive advisories improve your time management. As you arrange your day, week, and month, listen to your inner guidance. Sense the events and choices aiding the progress and completion of your professional and personal activities. You sense to:

1) Perform activities in a specific order. Felicia intuitively knows to pick up her dry cleaning, have lunch with her parents, and buy groceries. That specific order saves her two hours. Her dry cleaner closed early; she avoided making a subsequent trip. Eating lunch prior to grocery shopping eliminated impulse buying due to hunger.

2) Perform activities in combination. Terry intuitively sings, "The things I need surround me." The herbal store where she buys vitamins is in a shopping plaza with a new nail salon and ice cream shop. She gets a pedicure while eating a banana split. Combining activities saves her three hours of driving to former businesses in separate locations to purchase similar services and products.

3) Schedule activities at an earlier or a later time or day. Jeffrey intuitively smells pungent medicine signifying to arrange his golf outing for the fourth weekend in August. He ignores his intuition. His son's sudden trip to a hospital emergency room causes him to miss the outing.

4) Schedule extra time for particular activities. Roberto intuitively speaks, "This exterior paint dries slower than advertised." He disbelieves his intuition. He finishes the paint job an extra hour later.

5) Say "No" to doing favors for others. Derra intuitively tastes bitter cherries signifying to refuse to baby-sit her friend's two daughters for twenty minutes. "I'll come right back," her friend assures. She returns home ninety minutes later and utters a sketchy explanation.

6) Take alternate routes to destinations. Artemus intuitively sees a rolling inner vision show traffic gridlock thirteen miles ahead. He maneuvers onto an optional highway to reach his martial arts class. He avoids a twenty-minute late arrival.

7) Go to a similar business location. Anne intuitively sings a Ninth Avenue song. That avenue hosts a department store boasting shorter checkout lines than the store she usually visits to buy the same name brand cosmetics.

8) Call businesses to verify they're open during regular hours. Jillian intuitively feels a sinking feeling that indicates to call her hair stylist. She finds out her noon appointment has been cancelled due to the hair salon's plumbing leaks.

9) Call others to verify they're ready to travel as planned. Courtland intuitively hears the word "asleep" before driving to pick up his twin brother for a scuba diving trip. He calls his brother's cell phone. His wife answers and says, "Corbin is still sleeping in bed."

10) Share tasks with others. Ferdin, a workaholic, intuitively smells vanishing freedom. He begins sharing household chores with his two preteen sons. Ferdin regains four hours of free time.

11) Shorten activities. Shannon intuitively tastes sweltering plastic signifying to decrease the hours he spends sending text messages to his fraternity brothers.

12) Take breaks. Rene intuitively feels a clawing sensation indicate to break from his work assignment for fifteen minutes. He returns refreshed and completes his assignment forty-six minutes faster than he estimated.

13) Back up computer files. Vanetta intuitively sees a flashing inner vision show lost digital files. She heeds her intuition and backs up her laptop computer files. She saves herself frustration and remorse.

14) Slow down. Pedra intuitively speaks, "Stop rushing." She ignores her intuition and hurries to church. Jumping in her car, her leather skirt splits down its back seam. She misses the 11:00 AM service.

15) Avoid time wasters. Nathaniel intuitively hears his inner voice warn, "Don't answer your front door." His uncle drops by to spend hours drinking and dramatizing personal problems.

16) Avoid procrastination. Rose intuitively knows to finish family errands before noon. Instead, she watches soap operas on her new 52-inch TV. Her car's battery dies. Family errands are delayed.

Numerous books and classes teach time management—efficient ways to prioritize, schedule, and perform activities to maximize your time. These techniques are useful, but your intuition guides you to alter plans, as necessary, to save you time, money, and energy. Follow your way in planning and carrying out your activities for one week. Then follow your intuition's way for one week. Note the results and how much better you intuitively manage your time.

Improve your time management the intuitive way.

IN AND OUT

From my home, three post offices are located within a ten-minute drive. I walked to my car one morning. I intuitively saw a flashing inner vision show the post office I should drive to—shorter customer line.

I walked in and out of the building within three minutes. Ignoring my intuition and driving to another post office would have left me fidgeting in a long line for fifteen minutes or longer.

73. Can I use my intuition to avoid vehicle accidents?

Your intuition alerts you to potential vehicle accidents seconds to years ahead of linear time. Trusting your intuition helps you avoid numerous accidents and remain safe. Pay attention to your intuitive messages that communicate warnings about hasty pedestrians, reckless drivers, dashing animals, road hazards, falling objects, mechanical failures, and adverse weather.

Have you sensed to wait a few seconds before pulling out from a driveway or parking lot and then you detected a person, animal, or vehicle racing into your path? Have you sensed to remain alert during highway cruising and you dodged flying rocks, oil slicks, or damaging sideswipes? Have you sensed to drive earlier or later to your destination and you missed a multi-car pileup, bridge breakdown, or natural disaster? If so, you heeded intuitive warnings and avoided many vehicle accidents.

Even if you don't recall having had such intuitive experiences, begin to notice your intuitive warnings. For example, you speed to work and intuitively see a rolling outer vision show a tire blowout. Intuitively feel pounding sensations near tailgaters. Intuitively hear a caution: watch for falling furniture. Intuitively know a neighborhood child will sprint in front of your vehicle as you turn a corner. Intuitively taste icy spots on dim roads. Intuitively smell leaking gasoline underneath a flatbed truck. Intuitively speak, "Roadkill twenty yards ahead." Intuitively sing, "Road rage surrounds me, but I am calm."

People tend to ignore intuitive warnings while they:

- Daydream, zone out, or doze off.
- Eat a meal or drink a beverage.
- Blast music or talk radio.
- Watch a portable DVD player.
- Talk on a cell phone.
- Send text messages.
- Rush to reach destinations.
- Rant about personal or work problems.

Examples: Intuitive Warnings

Intuitive Seeing: Mackie intuitively sees a rolling outer vision show a six-car accident on an access road. Four days later, he watches a gripping accident scene match the one shown in his outer vision.

Intuitive Feeling: Karen drives on a freeway and intuitively feels anxiety in her body near a billboard. This periodically happens for a year. One evening, she spots a motorcyclist speeding in the wrong direction and veers into the emergency lane to escape a head-on collision. Stopping near the same billboard, her anxiety fades.

Intuitive Hearing: Joe intuitively hears shattering glass minutes before turning right toward his residence. He speeds up and parks his car inside his garage. A hailstorm smashes vehicles parked outside in the vicinity.

Intuitive Knowing: With no physical signs, Alisa intuitively knows a van driver will swerve alongside her truck. She switches lanes and dodges a crash.

Intuitive Tasting: Vincent drives during a snowstorm and intuitively tastes bent plastic. He slows down and misses hitting children sledding in the street.

Intuitive Smelling: Jessica speeds to her mother's nursing home. Approaching a suspension bridge, she intuitively smells fiery oil. She exits the highway four minutes before an oil tanker slams into a guardrail and explodes a mile ahead.

Intuitive Speaking: Larry intuitively speaks, "My guarded driving is crucial this month." Without vigilance, his excessive cell phone use will result in a tragic accident.

Intuitive Singing: Cassie intuitively sings, "Braking for wildlife." Her sudden song warns of an injured deer lying in the middle of an interstate exit ramp.

Your intuition warns you about potential vehicle accidents to keep you alive and well.

RECKLESS INTERSTATE DRIVER

In 1997, I drove to work one morning on Interstates 495 and 95 in Virginia. I intuitively saw a flashing inner vision show a red sports car recklessly speeding across three lanes at the Springfield interchange a mile away. Glancing around, I saw no red cars driven near my car. I switched lanes to remain safe, in case my inner vision came true.

At the interchange, I spotted the red car and hit my brakes. The driver recklessly sped across three lanes and missed hitting my front bumper by an inch. My inner vision helped me avoid an accident with that driver and other nearby drivers.

74. Why is intuition unpredictable?

Intuition isn't unpredictable. It allows you to know surprising details pertaining to your life and this world and beyond. Listen to your inner guidance every day, and sense seemingly unpredictable occasions: impromptu gifts, spontaneous visits, impulsive marriages, cancelled meetings, frantic calls, and sudden deaths. Your intuition detects the footprints of events in the spirit realm and then informs you before the same events happen in the physical realm.

Sometimes an intuitive message arrives in a flash. Marc intuitively feels certain he'll drop the cup of hot chocolate he's ready to pick up. Janise intuitively knows she'll hit the jackpot when she sits to play a slot machine. Brandon intuitively tastes spicy news the instant he accesses his email inbox.

At other times, an intuitive message emerges with a wait-and-see banner. Days, months, or years pass before it's validated. Rosie intuitively hears her nineteen-year-old niece's inner voice whisper, "I'm pregnant." Validation comes one month later. Raoul intuitively smells the tickling scent of a job bonus. He receives $10,000 the next year. Destiny intuitively speaks, "My gracious auto mechanic lands in jail." Police arrest the mechanic for purse snatching the next day.

Do you wonder why intuitive knowledge drops in your lap while minding your own business? Everyone and everything are spiritually connected like hands held across the globe. Past, present, and future events are broadcasted on spiritual channels your intuition receives each day. Recall sensing a story about a relative or friend and saying, "That's too crazy to be true." Then the craziness validated itself near sundown. Recall sensing a story about a celebrity and thinking, *That won't happen.* Then it happened to him or her on the red carpet.

It's overwhelming to sense everything that occurs during your lifetime on earth, but you'll receive numerous intuitive messages about people, places, things, and situations. Journal your intuitive experiences. See how life is intuitively predictable.

Your intuition knows what was, what is, and what comes.

THE INNOCENT WALK FREE

On July 1, 2007, local police arrested a friend's son and three other teenagers for assaulting an unknown man. My friend provided sketchy details.

"I believe he'll get out of jail when his court date is set in August," she sighed.

I intuitively saw a paused inner vision show white letters spelling the month, July. "Your son will be released in July," I said. "He didn't commit the crime."

On July 5, her son was released from jail.

"When will my adopted son go free?" she asked four days later.

I intuitively saw another paused inner vision show the weekday, Tuesday, and I told her.

"My adopted son's mother signed papers to gain his release next Tuesday," she confirmed a day later.

75. Is it my intuition talking to me while I hesitate?

Your intuition guides you to make wise decisions about someone or something, at times, while you hesitate. During your intuitive pause, you delay your exhale and an intuitive message snatches your awareness. Your hesitation in acting on intuitive messages you receive differs from your hesitation linked to intuitive messages. The first is due to your doubt, disregard, or fear. The second inspires you, saves you time, and guards your safety when you release your exhale and act on your intuition.

Have you hesitated after a novel idea popped in your mind? Did you intuitively feel excitement and create it? Or did you procrastinate and someone else profited from it?

Have you hesitated after a co-worker asked you to work his or her shift? Did you intuitively feel a reluctant feeling and fabricate an excuse? Or did you agree and gripe about the excessive workload?

Have you hesitated prior to stepping into an acquaintance's vehicle? Did you intuitively feel anxiety and walk away? Or did you jump in and suffer an accident or assault?

The next time you stop in mid-sentence or halt in your tracks, ask your intuition, "Why am I hesitating?" Sense the intuitive answer.

Listen to your intuition during times of hesitation.
An intuitive pause contains a vital cause.

ANGELIC REFLECTIONS ON A LAKE

At Calloway Gardens in Pine Mountain, Georgia, I saw sunlight reflecting on a small section of water in a lake.

I intuitively spoke, "Photograph the water."

I hesitated because the greenish water nauseated me. I decided to listen to my intuition and snapped two pictures with my 35mm camera.

Days later, I observed how my photographs captured the sunlight's reflections on the greenish water. Two angelic images surpassed the ordinary lines I saw with my physical eyes.

76. Can I change what my intuition says will happen?

Sometimes you have the opportunity to change what your intuition says will happen. The green "go" light sparkles for a limited time. Be intuitively proactive—not humanly reactive.

Portia intuitively dreams that despising her brother's new hamster leads to an argument. She smiles in silence while listening to his pet stories and prevents a fight. Herman intuitively knows a rainstorm will drench him during his morning walk. He wears his poncho and stays dry. Tara intuitively smells a blue police scent near a stop sign. She stops her car at the sign and avoids receiving a ticket.

At other times, it's challenging to change what your intuition says will happen due to delayed actions, lessons to learn, needed spiritual growth, and the free will of all concerned.

Sheila intuitively hears a direct voice advise, "Schedule your surgery now to decrease costs." She waits a year; her health insurance deductible increases fifteen percent. Lars plans to vote for a mayoral candidate. He intuitively feels a wobbly sensation indicate a lost election. The candidate suffers a defeat caused by his money laundering scam. Mata intuitively sees a flashing outer vision show his grandmother walking into a glowing tunnel leading to the afterlife. She dies the next day due to a brain aneurysm.

Your intuition never causes fortune or misfortune to transpire in your life. It simply alerts you to events headed your way or events already in progress. Change the outcomes you can, if you desire, and recognize the unchangeable ones.

Intuitive alert! You can alter the ending of some events.

CHANGING THE OUTCOME

One evening, I intuitively heard an angelic voice warn, "Don't reach. You'll injure yourself." I'd started to set a rectangular container holding cleaning products on the shelf mounted above the washer and dryer in my laundry room. The shelf rested two feet above my head.

I heeded the intuitive warning—no straining or causing cleaning products to hit my head. I grabbed a footstool, stood on it, and glided the container back on the shelf. I stayed injury-free.

RECOGNIZING THE OUTCOME

In September 2004, I intuitively dreamed my uncle and aunt visited my parents' home. My aunt remained inside their truck; my uncle rushed through the front door and into the kitchen. I neither saw the person he talked to nor heard what he said. Yet, I sensed he told someone he'd die soon. (My aunt died in the 1980s.)

He returned to their truck and drove off without saying goodbye. In the western sky, I witnessed an ominous cloud roll over the Tennessee County he lived in.

Months later, I called him after I found out he'd been hospitalized due to colon cancer. Based on my intuitive dream and a subsequent one, his earthly departure drew near. In September 2005, he passed away.

77. What is psychological anxiety vs. intuitive anxiety?

In general, anxiety is a normal reaction to challenges (e.g., exams, competitions, crowds), stressors (e.g., obligations, workloads, break-ups), and stimulants (e.g., sugar, caffeine, alcohol). Psychological anxiety is your mental response to imagined or real danger, and it's accompanied by physical effects: trembling, sweating, nausea, weakness, and/or fatigue. Intuitive anxiety is your inner response to real danger. It falls under the gift of intuitive feeling and contains inner calmness or peace surpassing human understanding.

Have you dealt with family feuds, suffered a debilitating illness, or struggled to pay bills and sensed all was well? Physical observations report your situation as stalling or worsening, but your intuition says, "A favorable ending happens." However, your intuition communicates the truth about a situation whether it ends well or not.

Before or while you experience psychological or intuitive anxiety, ask your intuition several questions: What's the real danger? Who or what is involved? How can I resolve it or avoid it? Sense the intuitive answers. Act on the inner guidance you receive.

Intuitive anxiety is your inner alert system.

A PATCH OF BLACK ICE

In 1993, I drove to my job on a Sunday morning, along Interstate 495 near Vienna, Virginia. I intuitively felt a nudging feeling that indicated to slow down. The interstate seemed clear after a major snowstorm. I assumed transportation workers had competently removed snow remnants, until I hit a patch of black ice and lost control of my car.

Fear gripped my body. I thought I would collide with other vehicles—psychological anxiety. I intuitively felt a pushing feeling that indicated I needed to tap my brakes and gently steer my car. I heeded my intuition, but my car twice spun around 360 degrees.

In my spirit, I intuitively felt inner peace surpassing my human understanding—intuitive anxiety. *Why am I not panicking?* I thought. *I might crash.*

Events moved in slow motion. To my right, I spotted a distraught woman who thought I'd hit her mangled car lying in the emergency lane. I missed it by inches. I clung to my steering wheel and prayed for divine intervention. Suddenly, my car perfectly stopped inside the right lane and pointed in the right direction. I sat motionless for five seconds and heard no sounds, not even other cars coasting by. Fifteen minutes later, I arrived at work without a scratch or dent on my car or myself—a favorable ending.

78. Does my intuition guide me when I exercise?

Your intuition guides you whether you exercise outdoors or indoors, such as in a recreation center, dance studio, swimming pool, or city park. You sense how to pull off an effective and a safe workout.

For example, you intuitively see a rolling outer vision show you jogging on safe sidewalks. Intuitively feel an impulsive feeling to perform ballroom dancing rather than power walking. Intuitively hear your inner voice say, "Today yard work beats aerobic stretching." Intuitively know to swim alone to sidestep hearing a training partner's gossip. Intuitively taste cool water to sip, not an energy drink. Intuitively smell rubber weights to lift during warm up. Intuitively speak, "I bike fifty miles a week and feel great." Intuitively sing songs motivating you while performing calisthenics.

Your intuition also helps you sense when to:

- Start an exercise program.
- Exercise at a specific time on a given day.
- Be careful or avoid using particular fitness equipment.
- Be careful or avoid taking specific training classes.

- Rest in between different exercise types.
- Keep pushing yourself despite weariness.
- Skip or curtail exercising to prevent an injury.
- Increase or decrease your workout pace.
- Check your heart rate for your target zone.
- Work out during hot or cold weather.
- Work out at an alternative place to avoid crowds.
- Watch out for attacking animals or people.
- Warm up or cool down longer than planned.
- Visit a doctor due to a health condition.

Your intuition is your inner training consultant.

Resistant Feeling for Resistance Equipment

A tingling sensation rolled up my back, and I wondered how I'd irritated a nerve. I intuitively saw a rolling inner vision show me exercising in a health club on the previous day.

I'd used resistance equipment to strengthen my back muscles. In my chest, I intuitively felt a resistant feeling that indicated to stop at twenty-four repetitions as initially planned. I ignored the intuitive warning and completed forty-eight repetitions because I experienced rare exhilaration in my back.

The tingling sensation lasted a week and aggravated me. I stopped using the resistance equipment.

79. How does my intuition reveal people's motives?

Intuitive illumination reveals known and unknown people's true motives. Your intuition bypasses appearances, conversations, and actions to unveil why people say and do things. You sense their reason, for instance, love, goodwill, fear, money, power, sex, and/or revenge.

Has a friend asked to borrow your car and you intuitively knew his or her stated destination hid a secret rendezvous? Have people held "homeless" signs and you intuitively spoke, "They own many homes and want free money"? Has a politician expressed a debatable belief and you intuitively smelled a ploy for fame and power? Has a relative insisted on marrying for love and you intuitively tasted dollar symbols? For these and similar intuitive experiences, ask your intuition, "What's <person's name> true motive for <subject matter>?" Sense the intuitive answer.

Expect anything. Ulterior motives are pure, corrupt, or a mixture of the two. Some people are oblivious of their exact motives; others assume nobody knows but them. Sense people's true motives; make informed decisions on how to deal with them.

Examples: Intuitive Illumination of Motives

Intuitive Seeing: Phillip intuitively dreams a friend, Courtney, needs $400 to pay a late car note. She had promised to use the money to cover her son's daycare expenses.

Intuitive Feeling: Emily visits her Aunt Lucille and intuitively feels a pounding sensation. She senses her aunt's hesitancy to voice her opinions is due to domestic violence wounds, not a laid-back temperament as other relatives believe.

Intuitive Hearing: Carlo's best friend, Miguel, boasts, "I'm spending time in Australia, without my fiancée, to discover myself." Carlo intuitively hears his inner voice state, "Miguel took a hush-hush girlfriend with him."

Intuitive Knowing: Mandy intuitively knows an associate, Bill, invites her to lunch to spread rumors about other associates, to make himself look superior. "We are alike and will have a good working relationship," he lies to her.

Intuitive Tasting: Andrew intuitively tastes vodka while talking on his cell phone to his dad, Arthur, a recovering alcoholic. Arthur lies, "I attend late-night parties only to flirt with women."

Intuitive Smelling: Wanda reads a bottling company's ad stating its natural spring water promotes good health. She intuitively smells a moneymaking scent inside the company's filtered tap water.

Intuitive Speaking: Dominique's brother-in-law, Samuel, claims, "I prefer driving seven hours to watch my favorite pro football team." Dominique intuitively speaks, "He's afraid to fly."

Intuitive Singing: A former high school boyfriend asks Kera out to dinner. She intuitively sings, "Twelfth grade revenge soaks his brain. I keep my distance from him."

Your intuition reveals the true motives brewing
inside people's hearts and minds.

A HIRING MANAGER'S MOTIVE

I applied for a job at an information technology company and received a phone call to schedule an interview. It proved difficult to arrange a time suitable for the hiring manager and me. He became extra accommodating, though he had other applicants to interview.

"I'm doing this for you," he laughed. "I'll interview around your schedule. Let me know what is a convenient time for you."

His motive seized me. I intuitively knew he sought an advanced position within his organization. My technical knowledge meant he'd found someone to take over his massive work tasks. Already overworked, I withdrew my interest in the job.

80. Can I sense why a friend stops talking to me?

Intuitive illumination reveals the true reason a friend stops talking to you. From an intuitive perspective, it's irrelevant how long you have known each other and how close both of you are or were. People's silence holds explanations accessible by your intuitive senses. Sense the big picture.

First, clear your mind of assumptions about your friend's silent treatment. Then visualize his or her face in your mind's eye, or glance at a picture of him or her. Ask your intuition, "Why did <person's name> stop talking to me?" Sense the intuitive answer.

For example, you intuitively see a paused inner vision show a big green-eyed monster jealous of your career success. Intuitively feel a goodbye feeling that indicates your friendship ran its course. Intuitively hear the laughter of his or her new cohorts. Intuitively know your friend is depressed in solitude. Intuitively taste a concealed drug addiction. Intuitively smell astringent anger regarding your offensive jokes. Intuitively speak, "She feels neglected by me." Intuitively sing, "He despises my vulgar manners."

Once you receive the intuitive answer, sense if you're guided to contact your friend now, allow a week to pass, wait for him or her to contact you, or let matters be.

Your intuition answers the "whys."

JEALOUSY LIFTS ITS HEAD

"Why did my friend stop calling me?" a client asked.

"She's jealous about the improvements you've made in your life," I replied. "She has the aptitude to improve her life but chooses not to change at all. She wants you to stay as you are so she feels comfortable. Otherwise, she's no longer your friend."

"How can I help her see I'm trying to better myself?" she asked.

"She knows it and feels left behind," I replied. "Her low self-esteem and her not wanting to change suppress anything you say."

"Will she call me soon?"

"She'll call you in three months just to confirm you're still moving forward. If you are, your friendship is over in her eyes."

81. How can I use my intuition to change people?

Your intuition communicates intuitive messages about and for others but declares, "People change when they're ready, not when you want them to change."

If you sense other people's lives—family and friends included—are like falling stars, faulty parachutes, or derailing trains, deliver life changing intuitive messages to them when you're guided to do so. But they must choose to alter their beliefs and behaviors, or they'll crash at an inevitable place and time.

Clients struggle when I sense no magical spells to make a spouse love them or stop cheating on them, compel a child to break destructive habits or ditch criminal friends, force a sibling or roommate to find a better job to share expenses—and so on. Intuition communicates the truth, not false hope. In some cases, clients give a relationship their best shot but sense an inevitable crash.

"How can I change him?" inquires a client, the stressed-out breadwinner in her home. Her husband demands she adds customers to her business to bring in more income.

"He doesn't want to change," I reply. "He's happy with the way his life is and the free time he has. Let him know where you stand without backing down."

"It's hard," she cries.

"I know it's hard," I sympathize, "but it's up to you to change your life, change what you tolerate. Nobody can do it for you. Do it one situation at a time."

People are resentful, elusive, or hostile toward those trying to change their harmful ways. Using your intuition to force others to change could result in its deactivation until you're spiritually mature enough to deliver intuitive messages and then live your way and let others live their way.

Has a relative or friend used his or her intuition to try to change you for better or worse? If so, how did you feel?

Your intuition helps change the lives of people
prepared for their transformations.

DANGEROUS LIAISONS

A friend ignores her intuition while meeting men. She intuitively reads them like autobiographies—beginning to ending. We compare intuitive notes and validate the hazardous personalities of some men she attracts.

I discover she enjoys starring in sexual escapades that she allows to override her intuition. My intuitive warnings fall on blocked ears, even when a dangerous liaison became a convicted murderer. One morning, he called her and casually said, "I shot my ex-wife. Can I stop by your house?"

"No," she replied. But she thought he'd joked about the murder until police arrested him.

"I intuitively smell stinky feet right before the phone rings," she states, accepting the murderer's phone calls from prison.

"Why answer when you sense it's him calling?" I ask.

"I like talking to him," she giggles.

She must choose to heed her intuitive warnings and change her dangerous dating habits to prevent crashing at an inevitable place and time.

82. How does intuition inform me when to let go?

Intuitive advisories inform you when to let go of a longtime or new relationship or situation—personal and professional. Your intuitive messages reveal wasted efforts and unnecessary pain.

For example, you struggle to let go an old personal relationship. You intuitively see dreams show steel barriers or ineffective maneuvers. Intuitively feel a sinking or lost feeling. Intuitively hear a disappointing or departure song: "I Can't Get No Satisfaction" by The Rolling Stones or the "End of the Road" by Boyz II Men. Intuitively know to break the bond or focus on other responsibilities. Intuitively taste an unquenchable thirst or withered grapes. Intuitively smell a crisp defeat or burnt cause. Intuitively speak, "Giving up the infighting," or "Our relationship met history." Intuitively sing, "I watch love seep through my fingers," or "It's time to sail from a dead river."

Relationships fall apart and situations crumble for various reasons. When it's time to let go, you sense to move on. You have free will to keep going all-out, but pause and ask yourself, "How much distress can I bear and for how long?"

Examples: Intuitive Letting Go Messages

Intuitive Seeing: Carmen intuitively sees a paused inner vision show an impassable brick wall. She falsely believes a discrete approach will improve relations with her absent boyfriend.

Intuitive Feeling: Felix observes a clash between two business suppliers. He intuitively feels stomach knots indicate to step back. His interference causes extra problems.

Intuitive Hearing: Denise admonishes her daughter's gymnastics coach. She intuitively hears a command: "Fire him." She ditches his extreme training and hires an easygoing coach.

Intuitive Knowing: Mindanao intuitively knows his advice is futile in reconciling a family dilemma. He stops trying.

Intuitive Tasting: Brianna arranges a hotel party to raise company morale. She intuitively tastes the workers' cold opposition and cancels the party.

Intuitive Smelling: Milton searches for his biological father and intuitively smells fading cologne. Years pass with no clues pointing to his father's whereabouts. He stops searching.

Intuitive Speaking: Lora intuitively speaks, "I'm finished with my gossipy hometown." She moves to a large city.

Intuitive Singing: Horace intuitively sings, "No more free cash." He stops lending money to friends who never reimburse him.

Sensing to let go of someone or something and doing it save you time, money, and energy.

FAMILY HISTORY

I contacted a cousin, who resides in Arkansas, to obtain genealogical information she'd researched years earlier.

"I'll mail it to you," she stated and gave me her email address to send census records listing her grandparents, uncles, and aunts.

During our one phone conversation, I intuitively felt throat emptiness indicate that I wouldn't receive the information, no matter how many times I contacted her. I emailed her the census records; she never mailed a single document to me. In my heart, I intuitively felt a let go feeling that indicated to obtain the information from other relatives; I obtained details from elderly cousins.

83. Can my intuition tell me if a situation will end well?

Your intuition communicates the truth about a situation whether it ends well or not. You sense when a situation is manageable or out of control, is headed on the right or wrong path, is safe or deadly.

Do you sense to stay at an unlikable job a while longer? Your intuition informs you that your next job choices are similar to or worse than your current position. Or extra time is needed for you to obtain a better job. Or quitting causes you to lose vital benefits. If you quit your unlikable job now, the situation won't end well.

Do you sense to give up a likable job? Your intuition advises you that your upcoming position supports your job skills or life purpose. Or it provides the time off required to pursue your dreams. Or it offers greater gains: lower tension, higher payer, shorter commute, and a friendlier environment. If you leave your likable job now, the situation will end well.

What's your measure for a situation ending well? It differs for each person: happiness, peace, success, love, justice, confidence, security, and/or freedom.

For any situation you experience, ask your intuition, "How will it end?" Or "What's the outcome?" Sense the intuitive answer. Keep in mind that several endings could transpire. For instance, you leave an unlikable or a likable job. Old friendships, routines, pretenses, and beliefs die with your departure.

Examples: Intuitive Messages of Ending Well

Intuitive Seeing: Lamont intuitively dreams he shakes a school board member's hand. Their divisive issue is mediated on Monday morning.

Intuitive Feeling: Sonja applies for a student loan. She intuitively feels warm breezes indicate a bank has approved her loan.

Intuitive Hearing: Kevin worries about passing the New York bar exam. He intuitively hears his deceased father's witty voice whisper, "Defense attorney in the courtroom." He passes the bar exam.

Intuitive Knowing: Faye intuitively knows she'll find a misplaced family heirloom. She spots it inside a hall closet the same week.

Intuitive Tasting: Clarence intuitively tastes smooth ice cubes related to his job transfer to Puerto Rico. His move is trouble-free.

Intuitive Smelling: Zena intuitively smells fresh roses signifying the healthy birth of her first child. Her family welcomes a fit baby girl.

Intuitive Speaking: Terrence intuitively speaks, "Money appears to repair my home furnace." His buddy settles a payday loan after a year of excuses. It's enough money to cover his furnace repair.

Intuitive Singing: Cassie intuitively sings, "I'm fired and rehired." The events happen two days apart. Another office assistant is found guilty of hacking into an organization's computer network.

Your intuition communicates situational truth—pleasant or unpleasant endings.

EMERGENCY ROOM LANDING

In 2008, my brother felt severely sick for days. His wife rushed him to a hospital emergency room. Doctors diagnosed him with diabetes. As he slid toward a diabetic coma, I prayed to God for his recovery.

"He'll be all right," an unseen angel said. In my inner ear, I intuitively heard the angel's soft voice. I intuitively felt inner peace in my spirit.

"He'll be all right," the angel repeated.

The situation would end well, but I kept praying. His condition steadily improved. Four days later, he walked out of that hospital and learned to manage the diabetes he didn't know had activated.

84. What are precognition and retrocognition?

Precognition is the ability to sense information—automatically or by request—about an event before it happens. It's a glimpse into a probable future because events change due to powerful prayers, lifestyle adjustments, attitude changes, and altered choices.

Retrocognition is the ability to sense information—automatically or by request—about an event that occurred in the past. It's a glance at a yesteryear incident, having no prior knowledge of it from official sources: people, technology, and publications.

To receive credibility and eliminate skepticism, share precognitive messages with others before an event occurs. Share retrocognitive messages prior to gathering facts.

Future and past events are intuitively accessible.

ARRIVAL OF A GREAT NEPHEW

In November 2002, I intuitively dreamed my teenage nephew's girlfriend became pregnant with their second child. The dream coincided with the baby's conception.

I told my nephew's father (my brother) my precognitive dream. His skepticism reigned. In August 2003, his grandson (my great nephew) was born.

CHILDREN IN THE AFTERLIFE

At a holistic expo held in Duluth, Georgia, I gave an intuitive reading to an unknown woman. I intuitively saw a rolling inner vision show her having two children, but they intuitively felt distant from her—two miscarriages or abortions. She admitted to the latter.

Wise souls in the afterlife, her children affirmed, "We hold no animosity toward you for aborting us." In my inner ear, I intuitively heard and repeated their intuitive message that shocked her.

The retrocognitive vision enlightened me to a truth: the everlasting souls of biological, adopted, and foster children—physically living or deceased—nestle forever inside the spirits of their married or single mothers and fathers. And physically deceased children can choose to be reborn in the same family or in a different lineage.

85. Why do I sense things when people come near me?

We are all spiritually connected like sturdy tree limbs, and we sense each other's life stories on approach and at a distance. People broadcast their life stories as though a high-powered antenna rests on top of their heads. And like a multimedia station, your intuition receives their broadcasted thoughts, feelings, and actions. Then your intuition communicates many life stories surpassing your physical scrutiny of people's body language, vocal tones, and behavioral patterns.

When people come near you, for example, you intuitively see a rolling inner vision show their peaceful or frantic day. Intuitively feel your aching feet point to their aching feet. Intuitively hear their inner voice state, "My energy rises higher at noon." Intuitively know their mood is friendly or hostile. Intuitively taste snacks they crave. Intuitively smell their family delights or troubles. Intuitively speak, "Their daydreams fly them to exotic vacations." Intuitively sing a song outlining their financial wins or woes.

Apply shielding techniques (see Question 44) to protect yourself against people's broadcasts. Multiple broadcasts may overwhelm you, especially while you're in large crowds: shopping malls, stadium concerts, and family reunions.

You sense people's live broadcasts near and far.

SCENE FROM A LAUNDROMAT

A young, smiling couple entered the Laundromat where I washed my clothes. Appearing genuinely in love, they cuddled and kissed near the dryers, after loading their clothes in washing machines.

In my inner ear, I intuitively heard my inner voice say, "They'll start fighting."

Within ten minutes, their embrace disconnected; their kisses turned into arguments. Then they hit each other.

I intuitively heard my inner voice say, "That's normal for them. They fight all the time."

86. Can my intuition help me find lost objects?

Intuitive detection helps you find lost objects (misplaced, dropped, borrowed, or stolen). Objects include electronics, documents, jewelry, money, and keys. They exist "somewhere" on earth; your intuition carries you to them, but some objects are irretrievable.

Take two deep breaths, then clear your mind. Ask your intuition, "Where is my <name the object>?" Sense the intuitive answer.

For example, you intuitively dream the object's location is underneath a sofa or by a gas station's pump. Intuitively feel a pulling sensation point you to its spot inside a pillowcase or lying on the front lawn. Intuitively hear an ancestral voice reply, "Check your upturned sneaker," or "Return to the café's parking lot." Intuitively know it's in a friend's van or at a donut shop. Intuitively taste a nearby item, such as cookie dough or cellar wine. Intuitively smell a nearby item, such as a bedroom candle or garbage can. Intuitively speak, "It fell in my cat's litter box," or "It disappeared inside a drainage pipe." Intuitively sing, "My sly dog buried it," or "It prays on a church pew."

Examples: Intuitive Detection of Lost Objects

Intuitive Seeing: Saratoga intuitively sees a paused inner vision show her missing house keys lying inside a wicker bathroom hamper.

Intuitive Feeling: Saul searches for his dropped black wallet outside a barbershop. He intuitively feels a tingling sensation in his hands the closer he gets to it.

Intuitive Hearing: Gabby intuitively hears the nickname of a college classmate who borrowed her blue and white jogging suit without permission.

Intuitive Knowing: Truman intuitively knows a cousin stole an old family photograph and hid it inside her brown tote bag.

Intuitive Tasting: Nancy intuitively tastes carrot cake. Her intuitive taste signifies her missing wedding band fell inside the carrot cake's batter baking in her kitchen oven.

Intuitive Smelling: Anthony intuitively smells papery numbers. His intuitive scent signifies his misplaced silver multi-tool dangles near his math books.

Intuitive Speaking: Lauren intuitively speaks, "My cell phone cries inside a co-worker's desk." She opens his desk drawer and grabs her stolen property.

Intuitive Singing: Norman intuitively sings, "A docile animal park." He finds his forgotten red notepad at the base of an animal statue.

Your intuition detects lost objects.

Refrigerated Keys

I mislaid my apartment keys. I searched every room and then rushed outside and searched my car front to back.

"They are somewhere," I said to myself. "I held them at the grocery store and couldn't have opened the front door without them."

I ran back to my apartment and scoured every room until I grew mentally tired. I walked to the kitchen and surrendered to a future finding.

"Turn around," I intuitively spoke—inwardly.

Nervous, I leisurely turned around. "My keys aren't in the refrigerator," I said, shaking my head. "No way."

"Your keys are in there," I intuitively spoke.

I started to dispute my intuition, but my right hand snatched opened the refrigerator door. My cold keys lay next to a milk carton on the top shelf. I grabbed them and eyeballed them, as though they had played a game of hide and seek in a spot my logic brushed aside.

"The key ring somehow attached to the milk carton," I rationalized, "as I set it in the refrigerator." No other explanation sufficed.

87. Can my intuition help me find missing loved ones?

Intuitive detection helps you find missing loved ones—adults, children, and pets. Physically alive or deceased, they're "somewhere" on earth; your intuition carries you to them, but some are obscured.

Take two deep breaths, then clear your mind. Ask your intuition, "Where is <person's name>?" Sense the intuitive answer.

For example, you intuitively dream your sibling stays at a cousin's home or in a hotel room. Intuitively feel a nudging feeling that indicates your friend's spot in a movie theater or jail cell. Intuitively hear your inner voice say, "Industrial park," or "Train station." Intuitively know your parents rest at a mountain cabin or in an emergency shelter. Intuitively taste a nearby flavor like an orange grove or a coffee house. Intuitively smell a nearby scent like a chemical plant or cow pasture. Intuitively speak, "My niece is lost in thick woods," or "She hides inside a closed high school." Intuitively sing, "My Rover sits on the Lake Erie waterfront," or "He's on the road to Ottawa, Canada."

Missing loved ones also arrange quiet getaways to unwind or be alone. They apply shielding techniques to block the sensing of their whereabouts—location concealment. They visualize protective walls surround them, or they affirm, "We're hidden until we return home."

Examples: Intuitive Detection of Missing Loved Ones

Intuitive Seeing: Ettica intuitively sees a rolling inner vision show her missing uncle lying unconscious in his home's attic. He'd suffered a stroke searching for antiques.

Intuitive Feeling: The Wallace family talks to an old neighbor while searching for their absent teenage daughter. Mrs. Wallace intuitively feels stomach butterflies and dials 911. Police find the panic-stricken teenager locked in the neighbor's basement.

Intuitive Hearing: April intuitively hears a phrase: swimming pool rescue. She spots her wandering three-year-old son playing near the unprotected family pool.

Intuitive Knowing: Matt intuitively knows his naïve twenty-year-old sister boarded a bus headed to Houston, Texas, to meet her mysterious Internet boyfriend.

Intuitive Tasting: Jan intuitively tastes burnt grass, as forest rangers search for her father who had vanished from his log cabin. After being struck by lightning, he's found lying in pain on a scorched hilltop.

Intuitive Smelling: Guy hunts for his missing rabbit. He intuitively smells pine and finds it in a vacant area lined with pine trees.

Intuitive Speaking: Ciara intuitively speaks, "Aunt May sits at 2100 Camden Street." She locates her roving aunt who has Alzheimer's.

Intuitive Singing: Morando intuitively sings, "Lights out in Copper Canyon." Police find his murdered brother in the canyon.

Your intuition detects missing loved ones.

SLEEPING BOYFRIEND

A friend worried her boyfriend had suffered a grave accident. She hadn't heard a word from him since the previous day. She left a voice message on his phone, but he hadn't returned her call.

I intuitively saw a flashing inner vision show him inside his home. "He's lying in bed," I said.

"He hung out with friends last night," she filtered her words. "But he usually returns to my home."

I intuitively tasted hard alcohol. "He drank lots of alcohol," I stated. "He returned home around 3:00 AM to sleep. He'll call you this afternoon."

He called her around 2:30 PM. She validated the details I shared with her.

88. How do I sense where to relocate?

Relax and ask your intuition, "Where is a great place for me to live?" Sense the intuitive answer. Act on the inner guidance you receive. Up to five locations provide the lively and free flowing atmosphere necessary to support your aspirations and life purpose.

For example, you intuitively see a rolling outer vision show a pictorial area exhilarating you. Intuitively feel an urgent feeling that indicates to move to a foreign country. Intuitively hear a town call your name. Intuitively know to deboard an airplane in a particular city. Intuitively taste customary cuisine. Intuitively smell native plants. Intuitively speak, "I'm home in <name the setting>." Intuitively sing, "Packing my belongings and cruising to <name the spot>."

You intuitively feel an irritable or restless feeling when a place is wrong for you. Relocating there or staying there due to lifelong roots, other people's opinions, or moving fears leaves you feeling miserable. You intuitively feel a blissful or peaceful feeling when a place is right for you, including an unvisited city or town with no close family or friends living nearby. You feel at home there.

View magazine and Internet pictures of the area you sense is ideal for your next adventure. Travel there and enjoy its amenities. Visualize yourself living your adventure using all your intuitive and physical senses. Let your intuition guide and protect you during your move.

Your intuition supports your relocation plans.

---

89. Can my intuition guide my words?

Your intuition guides your spoken and written words about yourself and for your personal and professional interactions with other people. Useless words shrink. Furious words injure. Intuitive words connect. They slide from your lips, pen, and keyboard with harmonious effects. Hearing or reading them, you and others announce, "I never thought about it that way," or "That makes sense," or "I understand things now."

Have you wanted to speak your mind, get stuff off your chest, or chew out an adversary by phone or in an email? Did your intuition advise, "Be careful what you say"? Did you express yourself and later wish to retract your words? Or did you listen to your intuition?

Have you wanted to hold your tongue, keep matters to yourself, or not topple the boat through social media? Did your intuition advise, "Speak from your heart with tact"? Did you stay quiet and afterward lecture yourself? Or did you heed your intuition?

Your inner guidance provides meaningful language and prevents retractions and regrets. Use your intuition to matter in your life—in the world. For example, you intuitively dream of empowering affirmations to use during self-talks. Intuitively feel a loving feeling that indicates to use doting speech to resolve family problems. Intuitively hear an adage: kindness wins repeat business customers. Intuitively know to type motivating lingo in text messages to your children. Intuitively taste prolific slogans to use for charitable fundraisers. Intuitively smell comical phrases to unleash at birthday parties. Intuitively speak healing statements to ill friends. Intuitively sing uplifting songs during international travels.

Your intuition guides your word choices to
convey the excellence within you.

Spiritual Experience

A friend shared details of a glorious spiritual experience he had while camping in the Tennessee Mountains.

"I want to go through the same spiritual experience I had then," he said. His eyes expressed a deep longing.

"If you have been there before, you're always there," I intuitively spoke.

My wise saying surprised both of us. He repeated my saying before I grasped its meaning: once a person undergoes a spiritual experience, it's embedded within his or her spirit and re-livable.

"I'm going to write that down," he said.

90. How do I use intuition at work?

To use your intuition at work, notice what happens with your physical senses. In addition, pay attention to the intuitive messages your intuitive senses communicate to you. What you physically detect and what you intuitively sense match or contradict each other. Your intuitive messages drop in to disclose the truth about workplace events. You sense the big picture and finer details about a person, place, thing, or situation.

Heed your intuitive messages as you enter and leave your workplace, during meetings and training sessions, while multitasking and daydreaming, in emails and discussions, and throughout breaks and lunches. You sense:

- Honest and dishonest conversations.
- Best, average, and worst business decisions.
- Hidden company and individual agendas.
- Project successes and failures.
- Promotions, demotions, layoffs, and firings.

- Building and workforce disturbances and dangers.
- When to stop working and stretch.
- Which documents contain valid and invalid data.
- Who will divulge personal dramas.
- Whose health condition feels as if it's yours.
- When electronic devices will glitch or shutdown.
- When bonus time or overtime goes in effect.

Worry not about judging or vilifying anyone at work. Your intuitive messages provide insights missed by a company's objectives, requirements, and policies. Listen to your intuition. Eliminate surprises and frustration.

Examples: Intuition at Work

Intuitive Seeing: Otis intuitively sees a rolling outer vision show an unruly business meeting scheduled for Tuesday. His previous vision showed an effective business meeting that occurred on Monday.

Intuitive Feeling: In her hands, Reba intuitively feels a tingling sensation indicate her manager procured useful products for her customer service department.

Intuitive Hearing: Bodie intuitively hears the word "firings." Within two weeks, six employees receive termination notices.

Intuitive Knowing: Brenda intuitively knows which business suppliers are competent and incompetent.

Intuitive Tasting: Artis intuitively tastes hot water. His Smartphone stops working after he drops it in a water-filled bathroom sink.

Intuitive Smelling: Brea reviews a monthly sales report. She intuitively smells fading ink signifying the report contains invalid data.

Intuitive Speaking: Everett intuitively speaks, "Opportunity comes now." He interviews for a management position and triumphs over a colleague who procrastinated.

Intuitive Singing: Misty intuitively sings, "Calm yields to pandemonium." A disgruntled employee attacks his supervisor in a lobby, and a frightened secretary calls 911 to dispatch police.

Your intuition is a reliable work companion.

ZONING OUT OF MEETINGS

I mentally zone out during unproductive or boring work meetings. My mind roams to faraway sites.

"Take notice," I intuitively speak to myself. The intuitive saying is my inward signal to tune back into a meeting before an important issue is addressed or when my input is needed.

91. Does my intuition guide me on foods to eat?

Your intuition guides you to eat foods best for you to maintain your health and stamina. What's best for you changes depending on crop growing methods, food reengineering practices, food handling and storage processes, and your age and lifestyle. Pay attention to nutritional intuitive messages anywhere you buy and consume food.

For example, you intuitively see a rolling outer vision show naturally grown vegetables to eat and reengineered ones to sidestep at a farmer's market. Intuitively feel a clogging (unsanitary) or unclogging (sanitary) sensation viewing meals on a restaurant's menu. Intuitively hear a motherly voice plead, "Give up salty snacks." Intuitively know which homemade soups are palatable or indigestible. Intuitively taste one serving to eat, such as a slice of cherry pie or wheat bread. Intuitively smell unsullied or spoiled meat while approaching packages in a grocery store. Intuitively speak, "No diary products for me this month." Intuitively sing, "Eating apples and pears sprayed with pesticide is unwise."

Your intuition warns you in advance to avoid eating foods harmful to your wellbeing, including dazzling and tasty meals. You can ignore your intuition and eat what you crave but anticipate consequences: a headache, heartburn, drowsiness, bloating, nausea, and/or an allergic reaction. Has this happened to you?

FOOD AND SPIRITUAL GROWTH

As you use and improve your intuition, you function at a higher frequency (rate of vibration) corresponding with your level of spiritual growth. You develop intolerances to certain foods you enjoyed eating recently or throughout your life. These foods now fall outside your higher frequency.

Valfred has enjoyed eating cheddar cheese since childhood. As an adult, he intuitively dreams he works in a cheese factory infested with rats. He awakens and recalls how his body struggles to digest cheese, leaving him constipated and belligerent. His spiritual growth calls for higher frequency foods.

High frequency foods include sun-grown and pesticide-free fruits, vegetables, and nuts. Low frequency foods include processed, modified, and canned goods. Examine your eating habits to determine the foods maintaining your health and stamina. Your intuitive senses inform you which foods will leave you feeling well and vigorous or sick and sluggish before you taste the first bite.

Intuitive eating saves you trips to doctors' offices and hospital emergency rooms.

EXIT FROM SEAFOOD HEAVEN

For years, I loved eating spicy steamed shrimp and crab legs. I lived in seafood heaven.

One midnight, I intuitively dreamed red shrimp sauce splattered all over my kitchen. The kitchen represented my health state. My intuitive dream warned me that eating shrimp poisoned my body, though no physical signs (e.g., itches, rashes, or paralysis) surfaced.

I began experiencing a sickening feeling minutes after a shrimp feast. Sickening feelings also transpired after I devoured crab legs. Reluctantly, I exited seafood heaven and became healthier.

92. Can I sense health problems?

Use your intuition to sense health problems for yourself and other people you know before they materialize or as they progress. Health problems include the illnesses, diseases, and injuries attributable to physical, mental, emotional, and/or spiritual causes. Verify the cause with a licensed physician or spiritual counselor.

At a fundamental level, you sense "something is wrong," or "an injury pokes you," or "a sickness stalks you." At a detailed level, you sense the cause without having prior knowledge of it.

For example, you intuitively dream about a neighbor's hip injury a week before his car accident. Intuitively feel head pressure indicate a sibling's menacing thoughts produce her migraines. Intuitively hear your inner voice cry, "If I eat that bistro's chicken salad, I'll contract salmonella." Intuitively know a co-worker's lung cancer is due to secondhand smoke. Intuitively taste a friend's raw heartbreak triggering her irregular heartbeats. Intuitively smell a sugary scent for a cousin with hidden diabetes. Intuitively speak, "The minister's pulpit gossip initiates his asthma attacks." Intuitively sing," My vice president is the sharp pain in my spine."

When you sense a need to visit a doctor or tell other people what your intuition communicates regarding their health, then do so. You intuitively feel a nagging feeling, persistent urge, or gnawing sensation—go signs. When you sense to remain silent about other people's health, you intuitively feel a resistant feeling, blocked feeling, or leaning backward sensation—stop signs. They know what's going on with their health, they refuse to know, or they are closed-minded to inner guidance.

Your intuition functions like a health alert system.

Corn Allergy

I prayed to God to disclose to me, in a literal dream, the food causing the itchiness within my body. I intuitively dreamed I attended a banquet and placed fried chicken and a yellow corncob on my dinner plate. However, the cob's missing corn spoiled my appetite.

Awakening, I realized my favorite vegetable caused an allergic reaction. I stopped eating canned corn and corn on the cob; the itchiness ceased. My doctor's laboratory tests showed no corn allergy, but I trusted my intuition more than test results.

Depression Enters the Circle

During a message circle, I glanced at a participant. I intuitively saw a paused inner vision show the heavy word "depression." In my bones, I intuitively felt a convinced feeling that indicated the depression applied to the participant's absent husband and not her.

"Yes, he suffers from mild depression," she validated his health condition.

"His depression will become worse," I stressed. I intuitively knew that she, a spiritual counselor, sensed he required long-term medical care.

93. Can my intuition warn me about danger?

Your intuition warns you about dangerous people, places, and things within seconds and up to years ahead of linear time. At a basic level, you sense "something terrible has happened, will happen, or is happening." At an in-depth level, you sense the specific danger prowling within yourself and in the world.

For example, you intuitively see a flashing inner vision show an arsonist igniting a fire inside a federal government building. Intuitively feel hairs rise on your arms while standing in a toy store packed with quick-tempered parents. Intuitively hear a police siren while walking to your car parked in a lighted outdoor lot. Intuitively know criminals robbed a convenience store seconds before your entrance. Intuitively taste back pain while hearing about an approaching hurricane. Intuitively smell a lethal scent after an innocent-looking colleague asks for a ride home. Intuitively speak, "I'll leave this crazy hot tub crowd to avoid an injury." Intuitively sing, "Speeding to a doctor before a heart attack strikes."

It's easy to doubt or ignore intuitive warnings when a situation is new to you or seems improbable to repeat in a hundred years. Your intuition communicates an alert before or while you associate with or encounter danger. The alert intensifies the closer you reach the point of no return. Choose appropriate actions to remain safe.

Rose drives on a road with minor flooding due to a relentless rainstorm. She intuitively hears a stern voice insist, "Drive slower." She turns left and heads toward her home. She intuitively hears the same voice advise, "Drive on an alternate road." She ignores her intuitive warning and intuitively hears the voice scream, "Danger ahead, Rose!

Turn around!" The two-lane bridge, six minutes from her home, has flooded. But shadowy moonlight makes it seem passable. If she tries to drive across the bridge, she'll reach the point of no return and battle to survive rushing floodwaters.

If you detect danger where you are or where you are headed, ask your intuition, "How can I protect myself?" Sense the intuitive answer. Act on the inner guidance you receive.

Examples: Intuitive Warnings of Danger

Intuitive Seeing: Malcolm intuitively sees a flashing inner vision show a playhouse component his three-year-old daughter chokes on. He confiscates the playhouse before the incident happens.

Intuitive Feeling: Jordan intuitively feels an uneasy feeling that indicates to keep a refrigerator repair technician out of her home. She cancels his service and later hears he assaulted a neighbor.

Intuitive Hearing: Watching a hockey playoff game inside a sports arena, Xavier intuitively hears an angelic voice shout, "Move out of the way!" He remains seated. Within minutes, a windstorm pummels the roof. Shattered panel pieces hit his head.

Intuitive Knowing: Destiny intuitively knows to board the next bus. Instead, she gets on the present bus. It crashes into a concrete side barrier on a busy highway. She suffers minor injuries.

Intuitive Tasting: Lars drives to a neighborhood car wash and intuitively tastes broken window glass. He turns left at the next junction and drives to a safer car wash.

Intuitive Smelling: Shirley spots a restaurant chain near a thoroughfare and intuitively smells a gaseous scent. She dines elsewhere and later watches news reports of a gas explosion at that restaurant.

Intuitive Speaking: A cordial, well-dressed couple enters a vineyard. Boris intuitively speaks, "Get out!" He leaves before they vandalize the vineyard.

Intuitive Singing: Talia strolls in a park and intuitively sings, "Stings on my face." She backtracks and avoids a swarm of bees.

> Your intuition warns you about danger like an
> alarm monitoring service.

NORTH GEORGIA MOUNTAINS

I planned to hike in the North Georgia Mountains with a newcomers' group. The Friday night before our hike, I intuitively dreamed to forego it—reason undisclosed.

After awakening, I still prepared to go hiking but intuitively felt a doomed feeling in my chest. I intuitively saw a rolling inner vision show me tripping on knotted tree roots and injuring myself.

My logic promised, "I'll be careful and watch where I step." My intuitive feeling remained.

I'd ignored my intuition enough times in the past to know unchangeable situations, no matter how I wished, strategized, or prayed for different outcomes. My backpack remained in the closet; I stayed home. I trusted my intuitive warning about the hiking trip and steered clear of knotted tree roots.

94. How does intuition alert me to important signs?

Your intuition alerts you to important signs for matters you focus on consciously and unconsciously. Signs spring from within you and reflect around you to answer questions, confirm decisions, solve problems, celebrate milestones, and impart knowledge. Signs pierce your awareness when you expect them and least expect them. Be open to unlimited possibilities.

For example, you search for a job and intuitively dream you check job postings on a former company's website. You query the website, see the same job postings, and apply for a position.

You drive to a grocery store to search for a hair shampoo. You intuitively feel your eyes stick on a new beauty supply store in the same shopping plaza. Stopping in the store, you find the desired product.

You sit in a restaurant and question if your volunteerism changes lives. You intuitively hear a celebrity's voice chant, "Well done." Then you overhear a customer's steak order: well done.

You intuitively know the cause of your health issue while reading a magazine article. You intuitively taste rapid success for your Internet-based business while observing sprinting clouds in the sky. You intuitively smell sparkling ink on your future college diploma after passing final exams each semester.

You pray for a devoted relationship. Then you intuitively speak, "A change in social circles leads to the love of my lifetime." You observe the word "love" in newly visited areas.

You wonder why you experience close calls while driving your van. Then you intuitively sing, "A distracted mind attracts distracted drivers." You become more attentive and close calls stop.

SAME SIGN, DIFFERENT MEANINGS

The same sign means different things depending on what's going on in your life. Interpret a single or repetitive sign's meaning for each intuitive experience. For example, you interview a third receptionist for your consignment superstores. You intuitively see a flashing outer vision show a billboard's headline: Great Choice! On another occasion, you add pinto beans to your dietary plan. You intuitively see a paused inner vision show a billboard's headline: Great Choice!

Your intuition clues you to important signs in subtle and obvious ways.

MISSION TO FIND A LASIK SURGEON

Wearing eyeglasses every day and changing my prescriptions every two years drained me. I set my intent to find the best doctor to perform LASIK surgery on my eyes, with no short-term or long-term complications.

I sat in a conference room waiting for my company's ethics training to begin. An unknown employee boasted about a famous doctor who performed his LASIK surgery five years earlier.

"I haven't had any problems," he smiled.

I'd heard a few doctors' names mentioned in the past. I intuitively knew the employee's doctor was the one for me and obtained his office number. He was unavailable when I wanted my surgery performed. But in my spirit, I intuitively felt certain that his recommended colleague possessed the same professional competency.

During my surgery, I intuitively felt a peaceful feeling that indicated everything would be all right. I continued to pray for success. The doctor corrected my eyesight to 20/20. Four years later, I've suffered no complications.

First sign: the employee's boasting pressed my gift of intuitive knowing to lead me to the right doctor's office. Second sign: hearing a colleague's name sparked my gift of intuitive feeling to communicate certainty for a successful surgery.

95. How does déjà vu relate to intuition?

Déjà vu is the familiar or eerie feeling of having already seen someone or something and of having already experienced a certain situation. Present moments feel like repeated past moments. Déjà vu falls under the gift of intuitive feeling.

Theories abound for why déjà vu happens. It's been attributed to wish fulfillment, double perception, a neurological disorder, a memory malfunction, a past life connection, or a parallel universe reality. Whatever the cause, many people report having had déjà vu experiences during childhood and adulthood.

Camille meets a young couple interested in buying her San Diego, California home that's for sale. She intuitively feels a familiar feeling that indicates she has known them for a long time. Randall intuitively feels a familiar feeling that indicates the gunfire he hears while reenacting a Civil War battle is the same gunfire he heard during the actual battle in Manassas, Virginia. Elgin visits Ethiopia and intuitively feels an eerie feeling that indicates he knows the main and secondary streets in the city of Jima, as though he lived there in a past century. Jade intuitively feels an eerie feeling that indicates she had spoken her eccentric poetry in a past incarnation in Naples, Italy.

Déjà vu—timeless replays sensed by
your intuitive senses and lived by you.

THE DREAM MEETING

I intuitively dreamed I addressed a minister I hadn't met in the physical realm. He taught numerous students in a classroom, but I forgot the subject discussed. The next day, I visited his modest office for the first time. In my spirit, I intuitively felt a familiar feeling (déjà vu), but he looked twenty years older than the minister I addressed in my intuitive dream.

On his small desk lay a framed picture of a man who resembled his younger self I saw in my dream.

"Is that you?" I asked.

"That's my son," he replied.

I'd met his twenty-year-old son in the lobby. No déjà vu experience transpired with him. It happened while I met the minister's younger self in a dream and then met his older self in person. Ironically, I stayed the same age in and out of my intuitive dream.

96. How do the chakras relate to intuition?

Chakras are rotating energy centers functioning from the bottom of your spine to the top of your head. Resembling spinning car wheels, they transmit, receive, and transform life force energy to support your physical, mental, emotional, and spiritual well-being.

Your intuition communicates information about and through your chakras. Each chakra holds a universal meaning representing different areas of life and levels of consciousness. The seven major chakras and associating intuitive senses are:

1) Root chakra involves security, survival, family, group belonging, and grounding. Located at the bottom of your spine, it vibrates a red color representing audacity, passion, and anger. The root chakra is associated with the gift of intuitive feeling.

2) Sacral chakra concerns your emotions, pleasures, creativity, and reproductive system. Located below your navel, it vibrates an orange color representing sensuality, sexuality, and joy. The sacral chakra is associated with the gift of intuitive feeling.

3) Solar plexus chakra deals with your personal power, self-esteem, self-discipline, and revolution. Located above your navel, it vibrates a yellow color representing intelligence, optimism, and integrity. The solar plexus chakra is associated with the gift of intuitive feeling.

4) Heart chakra entails love, compassion, unanimity, and empathy. Located in your chest region, it vibrates a green color representing balance, peace, and healing. The heart chakra is associated with the gifts of intuitive feeling and hearing.

5) Throat chakra relates to communication, self-expression, faith, and truthfulness. Located in your throat area, it vibrates a blue color representing creativity, tranquility, and freedom. The throat chakra is associated with the following gifts: intuitive feeling, hearing, tasting, smelling, speaking, and singing.

6) Brow chakra embraces imagination, visualization, dreams, and memory. Located in between your eyebrows, it vibrates an indigo color representing self-mastery, exactitude, and wisdom. The brow chakra is associated with the gifts of intuitive seeing and feeling.

7) Crown chakra supports divine inspiration, wisdom, power, and oneness. Located in the crown of your head, it vibrates a violet or a white color representing spiritual wisdom, transcendence, and astral projection. The crown chakra is associated with the gifts of intuitive feeling and knowing.

BALANCED AND IMBALANCED CHAKRAS

Balanced chakras allow life force energy to flow freely in your body. Imbalanced chakras obstruct your energy flow and afflict your well-being. Imbalances occur due to prolonged stress, poor diet, no exercising, addictive habits, unresolved trauma, and a negative attitude. Effective techniques to rebalance chakras include yoga, meditation, aromatherapy, deep breathing, color therapy, crystal placement, and energy work.

Ask your intuition, "Which of my chakras are imbalanced?" Then ask, "How do I rebalance them?" Sense the intuitive answers. Act on the inner guidance you receive.

Though chakras are associated with specific intuitive senses, intuitive communication carry on despite an imbalanced chakra. Your intuition continues delivering guidance to protect your energy flow.

A balanced heart chakra leaves Gladys feeling cherished. She intuitively tastes champagne while joking with a gift store customer. Then she intuitively sees a paused outer vision show the two of them on a dinner date. They reserve seats at a chic restaurant two weeks later.

An imbalanced solar plexus chakra results in lost personal power for Sonny. He allows people to treat him like a soggy doormat. He intuitively dreams about stomach ulcers prior to his doctor's diagnosis. Then he intuitively hears an affectionate voice say, "Volunteer at an animal shelter." Nurturing abused horses and whispering positive affirmations to them help restore his personal power and rebalance his solar plexus chakra. His stomach ulcers heal, and he stops allowing his fear of abandonment to render him a doormat.

Additional chakra information is available in metaphysical books and tapes and Internet articles. For the latter, use an Internet search engine and separately type in the words "chakra balancing," "chakra clearing," and "chakra healing."

Balanced chakras allow healthy flows of life force energy through your physical and spiritual bodies.

---

97. Can people more than fifty years old learn to use their intuition?

People at any age can learn to use their intuition. Learning is tied to recognizing what you naturally know. Intuitive senses communicate intuitive messages to people more than fifty years old as frequently and easily as to the under fifty generations.

People must discover how, when, and where their intuitive senses communicate intuitive messages to them in spite of their age. Those who are fifty and older, at times, believe it's difficult to learn to use their intuition due to a worn-out brain, settled disposition, or memory lapses—untrue.

The fifty and older crowd have at least five decades of intuitive experiences. These include sensing family member's health problems, their children's school ordeals, relationship issues, and financial hurdles. They simply must choose to recognize their intuition's communication methods.

Fifty-plus students attend my intuition development courses and receive private consultations. Highly intuitive, they freely share their intuitive experiences. No parents or other people are around to taunt or reprimand them. Most no longer tolerate such behavior.

Intuitive learning and recognition welcome all ages.

---

98. Are people born with a veil more intuitive?

A veil is a thin, transparent membrane or layer of tissue covering a baby's face or body at birth. It's a part of the amniotic sac encasing the baby inside the mother's womb. A veil is also known as a caul or hood and believed to represent a special destiny, spiritual giftedness, or good fortune.

I've met people who were born with a veil, including family members. In conversing with them, sensing their intuition development levels, and witnessing their intuition at work, I found them to be on a par with those born without a veil. People are more intuitive than others when they are naturally gifted, instill intuition development habits, have family support, and/or maintain open-minded religious beliefs with confronted fears (see Question 18).

Veiled and unveiled babies mature into adults who undergo similar intuitive experiences. They intuitively see wandering spirits, intuitively hear disembodied voices, intuitively know medical therapies, and intuitively speak imminent prophecies.

You are intuitive—born veiled or unveiled.

---

99. Are women more intuitive than men?

Spiritually, men are equally as intuitive as women. It's unimportant which gender is considered more analytical or emotional, weaker or stronger, the best talker or listener. When it comes to using intuition, it's listened to or ignored by women and men.

Women describe their intuitive experiences and their feelings regarding them in detail. They speak words, such as inner voice, suspicion, and hunch. Men seldom describe their intuitive experiences or divulge their feelings about them. When they do, they speak words, such as instinct, gut feeling, and "in the zone."

Women pack intuition development groups and classes seventy to one hundred percent over men. Women primarily purchase intuition books and tapes. Most TV and theater movies, depicting a real person or fictional character using intuitive senses, are starred in and watched by women. Yet, based on my life experiences, I find men to be as intuitive as women.

I grew up with five brothers and numerous uncles and male cousins. I spent eight years as an Army soldier and more years as a corporate contractor working with men of all races and ages. I sensed their intuitive moments during their stares, hesitations, brainstorms, jokes, and speeches. I observed their actions as if they starred in suspense movies. Sometimes I asked questions—one-to-one and not in crowds—to discover what they realized about their intuitive senses communicating intuitive messages to them. A few shared their intuitive experiences. They intuitively felt gut reactions concerning business opportunities and pursued them, intuitively heard truth and lies spoken during meetings, and intuitively smelled problems and solutions ahead of time.

I noticed how men, whom my aunts, cousins, friends, and I dated and sometimes married, used their intuition in personal relationships. They sensed words to say and acts to perform in romantic and calculating ways. They pushed receptive buttons, instigated guilt trips with precision, and whispered our desires—with charming smiles or serious faces. In hindsight or nowsight, we sensed their fluent strategies but doubted or ignored our intuitive messages to fulfill our desires.

Men knowingly or unknowingly use their intuition in twenty-eight areas of life (see Question 11) as women do. Listen while your intuition reports, "He's in the zone," or "He's reading you."

Women's intuition is in effect.
Men's intuition is in effect.

Veteran Hospice Worker

In July 2000, I approached a stranger on the first day of our hospice training at the VA Medical Center in Decatur, Georgia. In my bones and spirit, I intuitively felt a surefire feeling that indicated he owned natural healer's hands. His healing gift emitted vast energy in the training room. I felt I had to corroborate my surefire feeling, no matter his reaction.

"Are you a healer?" I asked.

"Yes," he replied, though my directness stunned him.

"I knew it," I nodded. I intuitively felt a distant feeling that indicated he'd told few people.

We chatted like two kindred spirits throughout training. I learned he's a Vietnam veteran and an experienced hospice worker.

Our hospice training ended. Beyond the material factors of the training, I sensed how women and men used their intuition to heal people, locations, and animals. In similar and dissimilar ways, healers directed their hands, eyes, voices, breath, and presence to carry out verifiable and permanent healings.

100. Are children more intuitive than adults?

Spiritually, adults are equally as intuitive as children. It seems as if children's intuition is far ahead due to their innocence and free spiritedness in chatting about guardian angels, imaginary playmates, and roving spirits. They seem to possess a stronger union with a higher power, in an increasingly open-minded world. They're given generational titles: Indigo, Crystal, and Rainbow Children.

Yet, adults were once children whose intuition communicated to them even when they suppressed it because of paralyzing fear, peer taunting, or familial abuse. Their subconscious minds stored past intuitive experiences, which are recallable by performing my Intuitive Life Review (see Question 19). Adults reclaim their inner power by acting on intuitive messages they receive each day and by reframing their past statements:

PAST: "I didn't know my intuition talked to me."
PRESENT: "I know how my intuition communicates to me."

PAST: "No matter what I said, nobody believed me."
PRESENT: "I believe me and validate my intuitive experiences."

PAST: "I thought it was best to keep weird things to myself."
PRESENT: "I help myself and others—weird things and all."

PAST: "My parents would institutionalize me."
PRESENT: "I am sane. I am normal. I am free."

Children learn or recognize how to use their intuition in clear ways matching or contrasting previous generations. No generation's intuitive methods are more superior or spiritual than another generation's methods. Use what works for you.

Lawrence's three-year-old daughter, Taylor, reads books and intuitively sees paused outer visions show her late great grandparents. As a child, Lawrence read books and intuitively saw rolling inner visions show his late grandparents.

Alberta gazes at window screens and intuitively hears her intuitive messages. Her sixteen-year-old son, Mitch, intuitively hears his intuitive messages from the grid—a universal network containing infinite knowledge and wisdom.

No matter each generation's methods of using their intuition, one thing is certain, intuitive experiences happen to everyone. Each generation learns to trust and use their intuition.

Adults' intuition and children's intuition are powerful forces in the universe.

THE GIFT OF INTUITIVE SPEAKING

My niece talked aloud to herself for years, puzzling her parents. In her bedroom, she carried on profound conversations with her higher self and spiritual beings.

When she was fifteen years old, I asked her, "Why do you talk to yourself?"

She replied, "I ask myself questions and then answer them." And she did it without thinking what to say.

She didn't wait for outer sources—parents, ministers, teachers, books, and the Internet—to provide intuitive knowledge. She asked herself questions and then intuitively spoke answers, unconcerned about other people's opinions of her custom.

Her intuition's Q&A sessions intrigued me in a familiar way. Our conversation led me to recall my gift of intuitive speaking activating in my teenage years with two variations: I intuitively spoke inwardly to myself, not to other spiritual beings and not aloud.

101. How do I help my children use their intuition?

Tell your children that it's all right to use their intuition—a spiritual gift from God. Create a safe and supportive environment to discuss their intuitive experiences. Let them enjoy harmless encounters with angels, ancestors, and imaginary friends. After frightening intuitive experiences, allow them to talk about their fears. Teach them how to protect themselves with shielding techniques (see Question 44).

Give them crayons, markers, or pencils to draw their intuitive experiences on plain paper. Explain their intuitive experiences as being a natural—not a supernatural—part of life. Read numerous intuition books and articles with them. Teach them discretion in sharing their intuitive messages with relatives, neighbors, classmates, teachers, and others. Some people misunderstand or dislike the intuitive messages your children disclose to and about them. Ensure the use of their intuition stays free of entertaining and impressing others. Such burdens lead to anxiety and resentment.

Start a personalized intuitive journal to record, track, and validate their intuitive experiences. Attend intuition development classes to advance their spiritual gift. Play fun intuitive games: Hide and Sense Objects. Who Calls Next? Name the Unexpected Visitors. What's for Dessert? Finally, remain a good listener as your children mature toward adulthood.

Give intuitive children parental love and support.

---

102. Can I discern other people's intuitive messages?

To discern other people's literal and symbolic intuitive messages, use your intuition to sense life looking through their eyes and from their perspectives—not yours. Compare it to pulling off your riding boots and putting on their boots, but you remain emotionally detached from them. Otherwise, your life experiences and perspective dominate and cause you to misread their intuitive messages.

What do an empty glass, a crowded room, and a speedy hurricane literally or symbolically mean to you? What do they mean to others? For example, an empty glass means a needed water refill to you, an unfulfilled wish to Sabrina, and dried tears to Lars. A crowded room means a family gathering to you, a networking opportunity to Nicky, and jam-packed competition to Dinah. A speedy hurricane means a fast-moving storm to you, a whirlwind romance to Frankie, and rash emotions to Octavia.

Follow the guidance provided in Questions 8, 9, and 10 to discern other people's literal and symbolic intuitive messages. That is, when they ask you or you're guided to discern them. People recognize your intuitive hits and misses. They say, "You're right on," or "You hit the mark." Or they declare, "I'm not feeling it," or "You're dead wrong." Either way, remember to pull off their boots and slip yours back on.

> Discerning other people's intuitive messages
> brings revelations of who they are and
> who they think they are.

BABY PUSHING COUNSELOR

During a message circle, I intuitively saw a rolling inner vision show a discouraged spiritual counselor pushing a baby carriage along a downtown street. I used my intuition to sense her life from her perspective.

To her, the pushed baby represented the ills of society. Certain clients depended on her to deliver favorable intuitive messages to them. Combined, they reacted like an immature, powerless baby who was unable or unwilling to solve problems applying his or her own intuition. She pushed them here and there and provided frequent intuitive readings to stabilize their soap operas.

"Set boundaries," I advised. Her stress had soared to a harmful level. "Break their dependency on you."

She nodded in agreement, but I intuitively knew she'd continue pushing that baby carriage. Underneath all the dependencies, she felt needed by them and liked receiving the money they paid her for intuitive readings.

103. How do I sense when to give others messages?

You sense to give people you know and strangers intuitive messages when you intuitively feel a nagging feeling, persistent urge, or gnawing sensation to do it. At times, you want to "let them be" or "not get involved." Yet, you deliberate the best way to deliver pleasant and unpleasant intuitive messages—time-critical or not.

Jonathan intuitively feels a nagging feeling that indicates to tell his friend to slow down while driving his motorcycle to avoid a serious accident. Faith intuitively feels a persistent urge indicate to explain to her sister how her custom furniture arrives the week after their parents' visit. Marcus intuitively feels a gnawing sensation indicate to encourage his mimicking girlfriend to audition for a role in a street play before the opportunity passes.

INTUITIVE MESSAGE DELIVERY

Your intuitive messages for other people regularly come "out of the blue." You might ask, "Why did I receive those details for him?" Or "Why do I need to tell her that news?" People ask for divine signs to comprehend and resolve things happening in their lives. God chose you as a divine messenger because you're the person most likely to follow through. Intuitive message delivery requires courage and resilience that strengthen over time. You intuitively feel relief or peace after informing them, including for dire situations. But remorse finds you when you ignore even wonderful intuitive messages to deliver to other people.

How people react is uncontrollable. Their resistance or rejection is normal, especially for intuitive messages that protect their wellbeing. Some people become worried, frightened, or angry. They believe you sense undisclosed details about their lives, invade their privacy, and spy on them. Others appreciate you and thank you for caring about them. How you react is controllable.

The more intuitive messages you deliver to other people, the more your confidence soars with three essential elements:

1) Discretion: Ask message recipients to step aside or away from crowds and then disclose personal details. Or call them. They're less upset and defensive when you deliver intuitive messages in private.

2) Compassion: Show kindness to message recipients whether they accept or reject your insights. Your intuition reveals who they truly are and what they truly think, feel, and do. Their truth broadcasts live and sometimes before they realize it.

3) Consequences: Tell message recipients the cost of listening to or ignoring intuitive messages—no understatements or exaggerations. Whether they believe or doubt you, you've fulfilled your mission as a divine messenger.

TO SHARE OR NOT TO SHARE

Not every intuitive message you receive about others is intended for sharing. You intuitively feel a resistant feeling, a pulling sensation, or stomach knots to remain silent. Some intuitive messages are only for your knowledge and protection or to teach you how we're all spiritually connected like billions of puzzle pieces.

Helga intuitively feels a resistant feeling that indicates to hide the reason for her brother's Christmas Day absence from their parents. Camden intuitively feels a pulling sensation indicate to hush telling a friendly stranger, a freed carjacker, about his black sports car. Noreen intuitively feels stomach knots indicate to avoid publicizing her prophetic dreams about church members.

Intuitive message delivery is part of the divine plan
to help people take charge of their lives.

NEXT DAY DELIVERY

I have given thousands of intuitive messages for twenty years and received marvelous reactions. A few message recipients acted skeptical or displeased when I didn't say things they desired to hear concerning their careers, finances, and personal relationships.

"I'm simply the messenger," I said. "I deliver what I sense and nothing else. Do whatever you want."

Once I intuitively dreamed that my best friend's relationship ended. I resisted telling her dismal details—not my business. In the dream, her boyfriend stepped inside two bedrooms that turned arctic cold. She covered him with a blue blanket and then stepped outside the front door. She brushed dirt off her brown hiking boots.

I awoke shivering from his coldness. The dream foretold their last breakup—a frozen death. She wrapped up their unhappy relationship and stepped outside to dust off her boots and go hiking—to move on with her life.

The next day, I intuitively felt a nagging feeling stalk me. I twice called my friend to communicate the dream, but she busied herself at work and at home. I thought, *Why should I tell her? She'll find out for herself.* The nagging feeling amplified; I emailed her my dream's details. Relief swept my body. I had fulfilled my mission. Weeks later, their relationship died a frozen death.

104. What is psychometry?

Psychometry is the ability to touch or hold an object and sense previously unknown information about its history and its users. Objects maintain their own energy and spiritually absorbent substance: metal (jewelry), fabric (clothing), paper (boxes), plastic (electronics), wood (furniture), and glass (bottles).

People briefly or extensively hold an object and imprint their indelible and readable energy on it. Their energy contains mental, emotional, physical, and spiritual experiences. While you handle the same object, one or multiple intuitive senses communicate specifics about their lives.

Attend a psychometry class or obtain a friend's consent to read his or her object. Relax and hold the object in your left or right hand or against your forehead or solar plexus. Or touch it with another part of your body: shoulder, elbow, or foot. Use one or multiple intuitive senses to detect information. Ask your friend for validations.

Homer sits in his mother's fireside chair and intuitively knows she plans a Hawaiian vacation. Juanita borrows a stranger's ink pen and intuitively feels his sinus infection. Marlon clutches an antique sword and intuitively sings a war ballad for a courageous soldier. They sense specifics that are later validated.

Intuitives use psychometry, a valuable tool, in artwork authentications, archaeological missions, and criminal investigations. Psychometry is used to read an object's past, present, and future.

Brooke sits at her brother's dining room table. Her elbows touch the tabletop. She intuitively hears amiable dinner conversations from the previous night—past. She intuitively knows her cheerful brother detests his wife's underground affair—present. She intuitively feels a distant feeling that indicates a divorce during winter—future.

Touching an old object (e.g., picture, gown, watch) or a new object (e.g., hat, bracelet, computer) affects your thoughts, mood, and well-being. This transpires when you absorb other people's mental, emotional, physical, and spiritual experiences as if they belong exclusively to you. Awareness is crucial. Spiritually shield yourself at home and in the world (see Question 44).

Touch an object and sense its hidden stories.

A Silver Ring for Two

I attended a psychometry class at a metaphysical store in Atlanta, Georgia. After an instructor-led meditation, I selected an ordinary silver ring from a covered basket without knowing who owned it.

Holding the silver ring in my right hand, I intuitively saw two rolling inner visions. My first vision showed a painful childhood event for a male participant. My second vision showed active spiritual gifts for another male participant. I described my visions, which the men validated and explained, "The store owns the ring, not us." Both men, store employees, had handled it on different occasions and imprinted their indelible, readable energy on it.

105. What is intuitive touch?

Intuitive touch is the ability to touch or hold people and sense previously unknown information about them. This ability—intended or accidental—is akin to psychometry.

People's energy is readable during brief contact: a handshake, kiss, or hug. People's energy is also readable during extensive contact: a massage, physical therapy, or intimacy. It's irrelevant which body part makes the contact. Your entire body possesses sensory receptors that function like satellite receivers recording people's life stories. With intuitive touch, your intuitive senses communicate their mental, emotional, physical, and spiritual experiences.

Abbie shakes a new employee's hand. She intuitively sees a paused inner vision show a red resignation letter. The employee resigns from his job position a week later. Jamie accidentally steps on the sandals of an airport shuttle bus rider and intuitively hears goodwill rhymes. His apology leads to the elderly rider discussing her missionary work.

Thedora hugs her spouse and intuitively knows he suffers heartburn. He describes the peppery pasta he ate for lunch.

Attend an intuitive touch workshop or obtain a relative's consent to read him or her by your "touch." Relax and hold your relative's left or right hand in your hands or give him or her a hug for five to ten seconds. Use one or multiple intuitive senses to detect information. Ask your relative for validations.

Intuitives use the intuitive touch, a valuable tool, in social circles, at business events, and in legal proceedings. Intuitive touch is used to read people's past, present, and future. Alternatively, people's energy is readable without touching them or standing in their presence.

Avoid spying on people's lives or exposing private information to entertain yourself or humiliate them. When details arrive, keep them confidential, unless you're guided to reveal them for a divine purpose (see Question 103). Touching other people influences your thoughts, mood, and wellbeing. This transpires when you absorb people's mental, emotional, physical, and spiritual experiences as if they belong exclusively to you. Awareness is crucial. Spiritually shield yourself in the world and at home (see Question 44).

Your intuitive touch gathers people insights.

Angry Airplane Passenger

A large man sat in a commercial airplane's seat next to mine. His right arm brushed my left arm. Instantly, I intuitively knew he loathed his life. I mentally blocked my intuition from sensing his private details. I removed my arm from the armrest to give him extra room. He'd partially commandeered it, anyway.

I started reading a book. In my temporal lobes, I intuitively heard a serene voice say, "Talk to him and he'll move his arm." I mentioned news headlines. He smiled, commented on the news, and released the armrest. I intuitively felt his energy shift from negative to positive. I used a shielding technique, prayer, to protect me from sensing his and other passengers' private issues.

106. What is scrying?

Scrying is the ability to see—intuitively—images in reflective, translucent, and other media: crystals, mirrors, gemstones, smoke, water, and fire. No scrying media is superior to another media. Utilize what works best for you. Literal or symbolic images materialize on media surfaces and reveal insights about the past, present, and future.

Mindy relaxes on a coastal beach. In the cloudy sky, she intuitively sees flashing images show her three-year-old son's daycare activities. Chase polishes his metal motorcycle helmet. On his helmet, he intuitively sees a rolling image show his August block party. Tavia creates glass murals for many clients. On the murals, she intuitively sees rolling images show her spiritual growth. Reilly builds family campfires. In rising flames, he intuitively sees paused images show the jubilant faces of his present and future grandchildren. Flashing, rolling, and paused images hold meanings for each person.

To perform scrying, ensure no materials or dust cover your chosen media. Release ideas about what you'll intuitively see. Relax and deeply breathe for a moment with your eyes closed. Then open your eyes, gaze at your media, and ask your intuition questions. Maintain your focus. Allow distractions to come and depart. Flashing, paused, or rolling images show you information about people, places, things, and situations. Notice if your other intuitive senses communicate intuitive messages to you.

Scrying occurs automatically or on purpose whether you are fully conscious or you go into a self-induced trance. Perform scrying on a different day when your physical eyes aren't tired, itchy, or strained.

Your intuition communicates intuitive messages using the surfaces of natural and human-made objects.

---

107. What is a medical intuitive?

A medical intuitive is a person with the ability to scan energetically the human body, in part or as a whole. Wellness, pregnancies, imbalances, illnesses, diseases, and injuries are sensed. A medical intuitive also senses if the source of a person's unhealthiness is mental, emotional, physical, and/or spiritual. Intuitive scanning is performed remotely or face-to-face.

Gene intuitively sees a paused outer vision show a man's throat inflammation. Jessica intuitively feels a teenager's skin infection is due to emotional trauma. Mario intuitively hears the name of a child's allergy. Regina intuitively knows a foodborne illness affects a school's cafeteria staff. Miguel intuitively tastes chest pain signifying his widowed mother's broken heart. Lillie intuitively smells a disease spreading in three nurses' abdomens. Bridgett intuitively speaks, "Gloomy talk produces a hormonal imbalance for my baby brother." Edmund intuitively sings, "My aunt is having a baby boy and girl."

Some medical intuitives are licensed doctors or work with doctors who confirm their findings using medical technology (e.g., echocardiogram, MRI, x-ray). Their collaboration prevents allegations and lawsuits when a client stops prescribed treatments because a medical intuitive's finding paints a healthier picture than a doctor's diagnosis. Medical intuitives can't legally diagnose or treat people's health conditions, but they can impart valuable insights. Their findings and doctors' diagnoses should match but may differ due to either party's inexperience, negligence, and/or egotism. Defective medical equipment also results in mismatches.

Are you a medical intuitive? Have you sensed people's health conditions before knowing about them?

Medical intuitives sense health issues and causes.

HANDS-ON HEALING SESSIONS

Medical intuition remained inconceivable to me until an astonishing event occurred in 1999, in Atlanta, Georgia. During an intuition development class, with a hands-on healing session, I reluctantly touched a participant's legs in the name of teamwork. In my temporal lobes, I intuitively heard two words "circulation problems." Startled, I hadn't expected to sense anything.

The five-minute healing session ended. Overwhelmed and nauseated, I inched back to my seat on the sofa. "I don't like touching people," I told the instructor. "I receive too much information about them."

My outburst released a personal revelation to me. For many years, I wondered why touching people unnerved me and raised my body's temperature. That one healing session pierced my awareness.

Class participants asked me, "What did you sense for her?" I gazed at the woman who gave me permission to tell her truth. I intuitively knew she doubted I'd sensed anything, except what she'd shared. I revealed her blood circulation problems, arguments with her mother, and other sore matters. She nodded with a stunned expression on her face.

During a separate healing session, I touched another participant's stomach. I intuitively felt her body's strain and intuitively tasted an acidic trace—family troubles.

"Do you have an ulcer?" I asked, stepping back from the healing table.

"I had one," she replied. "It's gone."

I remained silent to prevent causing an argument. She still had the ulcer.

108. What is an intuitive investigator?

An intuitive investigator applies his or her intuition to find missing people—physically living or deceased—and solve crimes, including scams, robberies, and murders. An intuitive investigator often works with the victim's family and local police. The collaboration prevents "suspect" accusations when accurate case details, initially known by criminals, are presented to police. Ultimately, an intuitive investigator's findings and police evidence should match but may differ due to either party's inexperience or distrust, missing or damaged forensics data, and/or mistaken or corrupt eyewitnesses.

Intuitive investigators work with or without utilizing metaphysical tools, such as cards, pendulums, and psychometry. The latter requires intuitive investigators to hold a victim's or a criminal's material possession, such as a hairbrush, T-shirt, or wristwatch. The material possession contains his or her indelible and readable energy imprinted on the object (see Question 104).

Clark intuitively dreams about an assault happening inside a cruise ship. Manuela intuitively feels a stabbing sensation duplicate a homebound man's cause of death. Salvador holds a missing woman's earrings and intuitively hears her rustic location. Delores holds a home intruder's broken necklace and intuitively knows his name and hangouts. Paulo intuitively tastes a hedge fund manager's financial scam.

Anne intuitively smells a bank robber's hot money trail. David holds an office building's ashy brick and intuitively speaks, "Serial arsonist here." Jasmine intuitively sings, "A stolen blue pickup truck sinks to a lake's bottom."

Are you an intuitive investigator? Have you sensed a missing person's fate or location? Have you sensed details to solve recent or cold police cases?

Intuitive investigators sense details of victims and villains.

MURDERER ON TV NEWS - EAST COAST

In the 1990s, I watched a Maryland TV news broadcast show a mother's frenzied search for her missing teenage daughter. As the distraught mother spoke to a news reporter, I intuitively felt a sinking feeling that indicated my eyes beheld the murderer. I fought my intuitive feeling in vain.

Two weeks later, Maryland police recovered the girl's body from a wooded area and proved her mother had killed her. I intuitively felt a confrontational feeling that indicated the mother had been violently envious of her own daughter.

I asked myself, "How do I know facts about a crime when I've never met the victim or perpetrator?" I began to understand the power of using my intuition to sense beautiful and horrific truth about people, places, things, and situations—up close and far away.

MISSING TEENAGER - WEST COAST

I've helped police find missing people—physically living or deceased. During one case, a police department investigated a teenager's disappearance. I intuitively knew she was alive and well and had run away to escape her abusive family. I reported it that way.

Her location remained her secret. Months later, police found her alive and well. She'd turned eighteen and wasn't forced to return to her family. She chose to keep her distance.

109. How do I handle truth shocks from my intuition?

The best way to handle intuitive truth shocks is to expect them. Anticipate sensing pleasant and unpleasant details about people, places, things, and situations. These include sophisticated and wasted talents, friendly and hostile locations, genuine and counterfeit items, and clandestine agendas and wars.

Intuitive truth shocks are communicated in segments to prepare you for reality or as a whole to reawaken you to reality. If you resist sensing certain events happening within your world and in the world, you'll still receive intuitive messages about them. Everyone and everything are spiritually connected like bunched grapes on a vine. Truth stops in, resembling a welcomed or an unwelcomed visitor.

Pia intuitively dreams about her boyfriend's undisclosed prostrate cancer. Juwan intuitively knows a volcano will erupt in a city in New Mexico. Honey intuitively speaks, "My parents will lose their life savings in a Ponzi scheme."

Once you know the truth about someone or something, it's written on your face—in your spirit. Your greatest acting role hides your awareness of that truth. How long will you act?

Find ways to soothe your nerves and claim your inner peace after you receive intuitive truth shocks. Suggestions include prayer, yoga, meditation, chanting, nature walks, and martial arts. Ask God or your angels to lessen truth shocks when you're overwhelmed.

Your intuition delivers truth shocks to set you free
from clueless and counterfeit living.

AFTERLIFE COMMUNICATION

In 1995, my intuition revealed my ability to sense afterlife communication. "Why are the dead talking to me?" I asked myself in shock. I'd watched horror movies for decades and believed that otherworldly communication belonged to Hollywood's imagination.

I intuitively dreamed when loved ones signaled their transition to the afterlife due to a disease, illness, or injury. Days, weeks, or months later, I intuitively dreamed they were alive and healthy. They talked about past, present, and future family events.

In the beginning, I awakened with shaking nerves and racing heartbeats. I prayed for restful sleep. Then I experienced afterlife communication while awake. I intuitively saw, felt, and heard intuitive messages for me and for relatives, friends, and strangers. I delivered them to recipients, initially with anxiety.

In hindsight, watching decades of horror movies prepared me for my spiritual gift of mediumship. Haunted houses, rasping spirits, and invisible noises have thrilled me since childhood, but I never envisioned those events and others becoming normal for me. Praying, talking to close relatives and friends, reading, and relaxing in parks filled with trees alleviated my intuitive truth shocks.

I discovered physical deaths never dissolve our connections with loved ones. We're all eternal spiritual beings. I learned to accept and appreciate my spiritual gift. I witnessed how blissful and peaceful the afterlife messages made people.

THE NEWSLETTER STORY

In 2009, I read an Internet article about a woman who sensed "something was wrong" inside her breasts. Her doctor doubted her intuition, but she persisted until he ordered a mammogram. It revealed malignant lumps.

In my bones, I intuitively felt a surefire feeling indicate her story would help someone else. I included it in my *Discover Your Intuition* newsletter.

Months earlier, a close friend introduced me to a new friend while we volunteered at a women's shelter in Atlanta, Georgia. My new friend disclosed, "After reading your newsletter story, I intuitively felt it struck a nerve within me." She'd sensed a health problem but ignored her intuition. The story compelled her to visit a doctor who diagnosed her with having brain and breast cancer.

"Do you remember me?" I asked her the second time I visited her in a hospital.

She studied my face and nodded despite having undergone brain surgery and radiation treatments. I intuitively felt a gentle feeling that indicated she knew me.

The chain of events and who I had helped astounded me. Praying and talking to our mutual friend diminished my intuitive truth shock. Divine hands guided me to the Internet article. A surefire feeling pressed me to include it as a newsletter story that guided my thirty-plus friend to obtain medical treatment. The chain of events helped extend her life a year.

110. Why do I feel a high while using my intuition?

You feel an intuitive high while using your intuition because your energy vibrates at a higher frequency than normal. An intuitive high is a high-spirited feeling of elation and spiritual oneness with everyone and everything. A frequency is a rate of vibration expressed in cycles per second or Hertz.

Your intuitive senses are more powerful than your physical senses. You physically hear sounds ranging from 20 to 20,000 Hertz. Any frequency below the human hearing range is known as infrasound. Any frequency above the human hearing range is known as ultrasound. You intuitively hear sounds beyond defined physical limitations and without requiring physical sources. Your energy vibrates at a higher frequency while you intuitively hear sounds, such as angelic voices, inner music, and nature dialogues.

Using your intuition, sense who vibrates at a frequency higher, lower, or identical to yours. People functioning at higher and lower frequencies repel or unbalance you. It's challenging to talk to or hang around them for long periods. People functioning at identical frequencies attract or balance you. It's effortless to stay in their presence for longer periods.

As you continue to use and improve your intuition, your energy vibrates at higher frequencies. You spiritually evolve. You feel intuitive highs and fatigue until you adjust to each frequency—your new normal. This happens several times a year or decade. Use grounding techniques to maintain your balance. Here's an effective technique:

> Visualize a brilliant white light moves toward you.
> The light touches the front of your body.
> The light enters your body and
> extends past the back of your body.
> Your glowing feet anchors into earth's divine roots.

Use an Internet search engine and separately type in the words "grounding techniques," "grounding and centering," and "spiritual grounding." Select effective techniques or develop your own.

Intuitive highs lift your spiritual wings—fly and adjust.

---

111. Why do I feel lonely as my intuition advances?

As your intuition advances, automatically or at your own pace, you feel lonely due to four reasons:

1) Your invented self dies; your authentic self emerges. Your feelings, beliefs, and habits are replaced by new ones. Who you truly are feels foreign to your invented self.

2) You sense life's truths. Some people differ from your opinions of them. Places and situations contradict your analysis or memories of them. Things gain or lose importance in your life. You feel as though you tread among strangers and oddities.

3) You feel cut off. You have intuitive experiences nobody around you has dealt with or wants to discuss. You attend or teach advanced intuition development classes but make no lasting friendships.

4) Your life changing intuitive messages fall on closed ears. Family and friends continue their detrimental lifestyle without considering grave consequences. You, the high vibrational outsider, is ousted from their low vibrational spaces.

Many intuitives endure loneliness, alone and in crowds. Intuition advancing is uncomplicated or challenging; it differs for each person. Express your loneliness in a creative way (e.g., writing, drumming, sewing) to ease or release it. Proceed on your spiritual path without conforming to busywork, meaningless activities, or individuals and groups having no substance in your life.

Times are changing. More people are receptive to intuitive experiences and attend intuition development classes. Ask God or your angels to guide you to like-minded family and friends. Applaud yourself for having the courage to live the intuitive way.

Your intuition advances during seasons of isolation and inclusion.

Purpose-Driven Loneliness

In the 1990s, I participated in metaphysical classes held in Georgia, Maryland, Virginia, and Washington, D.C. A dear friend attended the same classes twenty percent of the time. During the other times, I knew no one at hand and felt lonely, though I met likable people. Making new intuitive friends proved complex, as we returned to our busy, fast-paced lives in different cities.

My continuous thirst to advance my intuition pushed me onward to additional classes, books, and articles. My loneliness contained joy; it possessed spiritual purposes: intuitive knowledge and an intuitive lifestyle for myself and other people. Ultimately, I made lasting friendships.

112. How do I use my intuition to sense auras?

An aura is a colorful or translucent energy field surrounding people, places, and objects. It reveals a subject's emotional, mental, physical, and spiritual states. One or multiple intuitive senses tune into a subject's aura colors or translucency and related meanings.

A subject's states change at anytime for various reasons: a renewed attitude, a spiritual rebirth, health improvement—and so on. As a result, the subject's aura changes.

Anna intuitively sees a rolling outer vision show her twenty-eight-year-old stepson's muddy blue aura change to bright blue. He renews his attitude and confronts workplace bullies.

Aura Colors

Aura colors contain universal, cultural, and personal meanings with positive and negative aspects. For example, a pink aura universally means love or immaturity. Culturally, it means spiritual sensitivity or an inflamed health condition. Personally, it means birth of a daughter or indecisiveness.

Aura colors also hold variations and intensities. For example, the red color means love, sex, survival, power, fear, and anger. Its variations include crimson, scarlet, auburn, ruby, and burgundy. Its intensities, like other colors, are bright, dim, dull, cool, warm, muddy, and dark. Rather than memorize the variations, intensities, and meanings of aura colors, shorten the process. Ask your intuition, "What's the color of <subject's name> aura? What does it mean? Sense the intuitive answers with the knowledge that a subject's aura contains multiple colors.

Javon snaps pictures of his deceased grandparents' vacant brown-bricked home.

"What's the color of this home's aura?" he asks his intuition.

He intuitively hears the words "dull gray, dark red."

What do they mean?" he asks his intuition.

He intuitively hears two sentences: "Dull gray means the departure of loved ones left the home depressed. Dark red means an unsolved bloody murder occurred in the kitchen."

Examples: Aura Sensing

Intuitive Seeing: Hezekiah intuitively sees a rolling outer vision show a bright red color around the heart of his girlfriend, Mariah. Her aura shows her love for him.

Intuitive Feeling: Flying to Jamaica, Angelica intuitively feels a cool blue color encircles the country. Its aura reveals a peaceful trip despite her previous hysterical trip to the same country.

Intuitive Hearing: Chuck sings in his family's church. He intuitively hears a phrase: warm yellow lights the pulpit. A guest minister's aura signals her spirited sermon uplifts church members and visitors.

Intuitive Knowing: Marcia intuitively knows her uncle's aura contains bright purple and white—head to shoulders. His aura colors reveal his spiritual conversion. He validates Marcia's intuitive knowing.

Intuitive Tasting: Damario talks to his teenage daughter about her report card. She groans and he intuitively tastes a dim orange color. Her aura reveals social anxiety depletes her energetic personality and affects her grades.

Intuitive Smelling: Evette intuitively smells a dull silver color inside her desktop computer's hard drive. The aura color informs her of a computer virus.

Intuitive Speaking: "Steve is having a grubby green day," Angie intuitively speaks. Her colleague's aura color discloses his jealousy of her job promotion.

Intuitive Singing: Teri intuitively sings, "My parakeet is translucent." Her pet's aura reveals its healthy state.

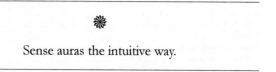

Sense auras the intuitive way.

Aura Sensing Styles

In the 1990s, I attended classes and read books describing how to see auras. No technique worked until I realized I intuitively felt aura colors as weighty feelings and sensations instead of intuitively seeing them. The accurate meanings rose with the colors. For instance, I intuitively felt an angry "red" feeling burst from a co-worker (family upheaval), a healing "green" sensation ooze inside an art supply store (healing power of art), and a serene "blue" feeling splash the sky (a peaceful picnic).

I met others who intuitively heard the names of aura colors or intuitively tasted or smelled them. Each individual's intuition communicates aura details in ways best for him or her. No aura sensing style is superior to another style. Classes and books that focus entirely on intuitively seeing auras miss many people. Eight intuitive senses reveal a subject's aura colors or translucency and related meanings. Everyone can learn to use any intuitive sense to perceive auras.

113. What is the difference between ghosts and spirits?

Ghosts and spirits are both spiritual beings but named differently to distinguish their dispositions and actions. Ghosts are physically deceased (no human body) and emotionally attached to particular people, locations, and objects. This is due to an endless love, a traumatic death, or unfinished business. Earthbound, they haunt or delay leaving loved ones and others. They feed on fear, hate, misery, and loneliness. Their energy intuitively feels cold, scratchy, or prickly.

Spirits are physically living (own a human body) like you and me and physically deceased (no human body) like ancestors. Earth-free, the latter occasionally visits loved ones. They give comfort, love, support, and warnings. Their energy intuitively feels warm, soothing, or comforting.

Ghosts and spirits materialize in previous forms when they seek recognition by loved ones and others who know their life storylines. They are physically and intuitively sensed. People having no knowledge of their earthly lives may be able to obtain verification by researching census, library, and courthouse records.

Ghosts and spirits materialize in photographs as themselves or as orbs, lights, shadows, and mist. Skeptics attribute the images to camera malfunctions or adverse weather. They reproduce similar images via trick photography. You decide what's real and what's imitated.

DETECTING GHOSTS AND SPIRITS

Your intuitive senses detect the presence of ghosts and spirits. For example, you intuitively see paused outer visions show their image in bathroom mirrors. Intuitively feel "cold spots" following you in your home. Intuitively hear disembodied voices at work. Intuitively know they hover near your vehicle's hood. Intuitively smell their lingering fragrance in their former home. Intuitively taste their airy flavors at family reunions. Intuitively speak, "Doors open by themselves." Intuitively sing, "Invisible hands turn my ceiling lights off and on."

Utilize shielding techniques (see Question 44) to protect yourself against frightening ghosts and spirits. If they show up in your home or follow your footsteps in the world, you demand, "In the name of God, let me have my peace. Be gone!"

Your physical and intuitive senses detect the presence of ghosts and spirits moving among us.

Georgia Farmhouse

Two people and I inspected a hundred-year-old Georgia farmhouse. A fourth person, the renter, talked about his terrifying episodes in which he intuitively saw and heard ghosts. Standing in a sizeable bedroom, I intuitively saw two rolling inner visions.

The first vision showed a young woman lying in bed and giving birth to a daughter. The scene switched to an older woman lying in bed and dying due to pneumonia. As spirits, they sporadically visited the farmhouse.

The second vision showed a furious man dressed in a long black coat and a black shirt, pants, and boots. He walked back and forth but stopped and stared to let me know he saw me, too. The man, a ghost, is emotionally attached to the farmhouse and revengeful acts that happened there in the early 1900s. He refused to move on.

Still terrified and exhausted, the renter packed his belongings and moved out that night. Nobody researched the farmhouse's history or talked with the owners about the spirits and ghost.

114. How do I know which inner voice is my own?

You intuitively hear many inner voices in your temporal lobes, inner ear, heart, and "out in space." These include your own inner voice and those owned by other people and spiritual beings: God, angels, spirit guides, and ancestors. God often speaks to you through your inner voice to prevent frightening you with a heavenly voice.

Practice and experience will teach you to sense which inner voice is yours for audible intuitive messages. Four ways exist:

1) Your unique, softer inner voice belongs to you the same as your unique, louder physical voice. Pay attention to how you inwardly talk

to yourself while feeling content, serene, and cautious. Your inward talk's tone matches your inner voice's tone.

2) You intuitively hear your inner voice speak inside and outside your physical body, and you intuitively feel its resemblance of you. You intuitively hear other inner voices speak inside and outside your physical body, but you intuitively feel their distinction from you.

3) Ask your intuition, "Who's talking?" Or "Who said that?" One or multiple intuitive senses answer.

Sharlene intuitively hears a forceful inner voice say, "Stop dancing. You'll get into trouble." She asks her intuition, "Who said that?" She intuitively sees a flashing inner vision show a woman standing inside an ice cream shop. Arriving at the ice cream shop, Sharlene physically sees the envisioned woman and her two-year-old son who twirls next to her. She scolds him, "Stop dancing. You'll get into trouble."

4) Note the focus of the inner voice speaking. What concerns you versus what concerns others?

Daniel shops in a grocery store. He intuitively hears a tender inner voice say, "Buy two dozen eggs." It isn't his inner voice or focus. He sees a young woman pick up two cartons of eggs. Then he intuitively hears an angelic inner voice warn, "Watch for spilled potato chips." It isn't his inner voice or focus, but he sidesteps broken chips scattered on the store's floor. Lastly, he intuitively hears a cautious inner voice shout, "Checkout lines are getting crowded!" His inner voice focuses on his intent to avoid long lines.

OTHER INNER VOICES

Other people's inner voice sounds like a softer version of their physical voice. Other spiritual beings' inner voice takes on a human quality or natural elements, such as crackling leaves, booming thunder, and howling wind.

If you intuitively hear any inner voice direct you to harm yourself, others, or objects, take control of those situations. Refuse to comply.

Spiritually shield yourself against negative energy imprints and entities (see Question 44). Talk to a trusted relative or friend. If needed, seek spiritual counseling.

> The communication of inner voices is sensed by
> those with intuitive ears to hear.

INNER VOICES IN MY SPACE

I intuitively hear diverse inner voices, including my own, at home and in the world. Most inner voices talk about current and future events. A few discuss past events. My intuitive experiences include:

1) I attended a crowded book signing by well-known author, Ernest J. Gaines. I glanced at him. In my inner ear, I intuitively heard my inner voice whisper, "There are few writers left like him."

Seconds later, a quiet woman standing in line behind me said, "There aren't many writers left like him."

My inner voice said what her physical voice repeated with a slight variation.

2) A client asked me what to do about her career and relocation plans. I'd earlier given her an intuitive consultation and taught her how to use her own intuition.

"Let her decide what do," her guardian angel advised. In my heart, I intuitively heard her angel's inner voice. I also intuitively felt a let go feeling. My client needed to trust her own intuition and act on its guidance.

3) I awakened one morning. In my inner ear, I intuitively heard a man's inner voice state, "When timely gets worn, we know what to do."

"Who's talking?" I asked my intuition.

I intuitively saw a paused inner vision show the blank face of a nameless man. Harmless, his saying meant that things happen aligned with divine timing and not at the time we want. Then we know the proper actions to perform to achieve success.

115. How can I slow my thoughts to notice my intuitive messages?

Six focus-shifting techniques decrease your speeding thoughts. These techniques help you live in the present moment and notice your intuitive messages arriving within and in between remaining thoughts. These techniques also stop you from replaying the past and redesigning the future.

Technique One. Find a quiet area. Stand or sit in a comfortable position and concentrate on your breathing. Inhale through your nose to a count of five. Then exhale through your mouth to a count of five. Do this two-step sequence at least three times in a row. Feel the tension release from your body. Feel your thoughts diminish.

Technique Two. Enjoy a relaxing activity: listen to music, immerse in a bubble bath, go horseback riding—and so on. Your activity captures your attention and reduces distracting thoughts.

Technique Three. Spend time in nature walking, sitting, or playing. Let your exposed feet touch the grass, dirt, and water. Your thoughts drift as you witness the beauty and wonder of flowers, trees, waterfalls, rivers, mountains, insects, and animals.

Technique Four. Use your imagination—a creative inner tool. Imagine your thoughts drag and stumble like a portable music player with weakening batteries. The batteries die within eight seconds; the music stops. Hear the silence inside your head.

Technique Five. Tell yourself a grand story. Create a setting for your intuition to save a child's life. For example, debris falls from a parking garage. You intuitively feel a pushing feeling that indicates to rescue a five-year-old boy. Narrate the scene, from beginning to ending. Your thoughts become quieter as if they are opera attendees.

Technique Six. Do vigorous exercises. Many thoughts exit when you perform high-powered activities: calisthenics, racquetball, juggling—and so on. Your lone thought says, "I love this," or "I'll be glad when this is over."

Incorporate focus-shifting techniques in your schedule each week. Notice how your thoughts slow down and how you reap twenty-one benefits of using your intuition (see Question 11).

Slowed thinking leads to heightened intuitive awareness.

116. How are energy imprints sensed?

An energy imprint is the residual energy of a pleasant or unpleasant event stored in a physical body (living or deceased) or spiritual body, at a location, or in an object. Each year thousands of events begin and end or continue. They leave indelible signatures or recordings, layer on layer, wherever and whenever they occurred. These events contain powerful emotions: love, joy, excitement, pain, fear, and hate wrapped inside stories your intuition senses.

For example, you glance at a foreigner and intuitively see a paused inner vision show his past occupations. Shake a birthday party guest's hand and intuitively feel her happy or sad childhood. Enter an aged mansion and intuitively hear long-ago conversations. Wear a cousin's

T-shirt and intuitively know his motive for his disappearance and reappearance five years later. Visit a historic town and intuitively taste its hospitable or inhospitable legends. Touch an antique dresser and intuitively smell decades of nonviolence or bloodshed. Sit beside an aged fig tree and intuitively speak its unreported narrative. Browse a family photo album and intuitively sing untold ancestral songs.

Utilize shielding techniques (see Question 44) to protect yourself against residual energy imprints that could ruin your life. If necessary, consult a professional energy worker to help you release harmful energy imprints of people, places, and things.

Examples: Energy Imprints

Intuitive Seeing: Caldwell visits a neighbor's home. He intuitively sees rolling inner visions show past family gatherings as if they occur in the present.

Intuitive Feeling: Lydia picks up her godmother's violin and intuitively feels grief. Her cheerful-acting godmother still grieves about an unfulfilled music career she'd pursued in the 1970s.

Intuitive Hearing: Lamar intuitively hears the exciting account of a gemstone he holds in his right hand inside a cavern.

Intuitive Knowing: Gertrude intuitively knows what happened to her missing German Shepherd and follows its two-day old trail.

Intuitive Tasting: Forester tours ancient sites in South America and intuitively tastes spices and herbs linked to previous centuries.

Intuitive Smelling: Ida intuitively smells a riveting fragrance inside an antique trunk. The fragrance retains the history of its nineteenth century owner.

Intuitive Speaking: Manny intuitively speaks, "My grandpa died of heart failure in 1967, on the exact spot I stand in this blue barn." His grandma confirms it happened that way.

Intuitive Singing: Sharon sees a picture of an ill coal miner. She intuitively sings a song about his final hours trapped inside a coal mine, a decade before her birth.

Your intuitive senses tap into energy imprints across eras.

CIVIL WAR BATTLE

I dwell in a historic district where a Civil War battle occurred in July 1864. I intuitively see rolling outer visions show an energy imprint: Confederate soldiers march by my dining room's window as if the battle continues.

An army officer stops and stares in my direction. He says nothing, then turns to his left and follows his soldiers. The Civil War battle, along with others, deposited energy imprints on the land it engaged during fighting.

117. Do angels communicate to me via my intuition?

Angels communicate to you via your intuition. They are divine messengers of God and provide wisdom, knowledge, comfort, encouragement, assistance, and protection for you and others. Pay attention to intuitive messages revealing the presence of winged and wingless angels wherever you are.

Angels exist everywhere. For instance, they visit homes, churches, schools, workplaces, hospitals, and amphitheaters. They are present on airplanes, buses, trains, campgrounds, playgrounds, and highways. Their glorious missions assist those in need.

Your intuitive senses realize angelic communication. For example, you intuitively see visions and dreams show angels appearing as humans, statues, or lights to guide you past danger. Intuitively feel bodily chills or feathery sensations while they impart knowledge to you. Intuitively hear an angel's name followed by spiritual wisdom. Intuitively know they protect you during natural disasters. Intuitively taste a vanilla or cinnamon flavor signifying angelic their support for your finest decisions. Intuitively smell perfumed or floral scents signifying angelic comfort during your distressing moments. Intuitively speak, "Their heavenly arrivals uphold my life purpose." Intuitively sing a rally song with angels encouraging you to achieve your goals.

Examples: Angelic Communication

Intuitive Seeing: In a courtroom, Peter intuitively sees a flashing outer vision show purple lights. The lights, angels, guide him to speak the truth to win his lawsuit.

Intuitive Feeling: Flora cooks dinner in her kitchen. She intuitively feels bodily chills signaling the presence of her angel, Uriel. The angel says, "A child arrives in your immediate family in ten months."

Intuitive Hearing: Gregory intuitively hears the chorus of the song "Angel" performed by Sarah McLachlan. His guardian angel protects him during his outpatient surgery.

Intuitive Knowing: Ashley intuitively knows when angels drop in to deliver intuitive messages about sick loved ones to contact.

Intuitive Tasting: In his condo, Zachary intuitively tastes burnt air. It signifies an angelic warning to control his hot temper.

Intuitive Smelling: Patrice intuitively smells sandalwood incense in her college dorm. Her guardian angel, Celeste, comforts her during a miserable period away from her parents.

Intuitive Speaking: Normandy intuitively speaks his angel's name, Gilder. He's guided past a thoroughfare with an unseen sinkhole.

Intuitive Singing: Khadijah intuitively sings stirring songs for angels assisting her with homeless runaways.

WICKED ANGELS

A few angels strive to hinder your spiritual/human journey. Wicked angels exist as do wicked human beings. They also communicate to you via your intuitive senses, but you sense their malevolence.

For example, you intuitively see visions and dreams show horrendous monsters. Intuitively feel a troubling feeling or sticky sensation from their presence. Intuitively hear their disingenuous scriptures or phrases. Intuitively know to avoid them. Intuitively taste acidic or callous seasoning inside their messages. Intuitively smell odious or toxic scents discharge from them. Intuitively speak about their ill will. Intuitively sing about menacing spiritual beings.

Their inglorious missions are to perturb or harm you, even with messages containing truth. Use shielding techniques (see Question 44) to protect yourself against wicked angels. Demand they leave in God's name.

Your intuitive senses perceive angelic communication.

ANGELIC COMMUNICATION AT WORK

I intuitively see small, large, or gigantic angels in my intuitive visions and dreams. They surface as themselves, as humans, or as objects. As the angels stand next to or move around people, their facial features resemble human features. Their flowing gowns contain lovely colors like gold, pearl, or violet.

I withstood an irritating day at work. In my inner ear, I intuitively heard an angel recite a comforting poem:

The tides are turning
There are no last laughs
For greater are you
Than the trying time that will come to pass

Then I intuitively heard the title of Rev. Al Green's song "Everything's Gonna Be Alright." The poem and song validated my day would end well and it did.

118. How does intuition work with the white light?

The white light is multifaceted divine energy or power that spiritually cleanses, heals, transforms, and protects you. It also awakens you to spiritual knowledge and wisdom. The white light shines continuously and flashes or intensifies to capture your attention. Its infinite range and alternating form are unconstrained by physical realm laws.

Use your intuition to draw on the white light or sense its divine mission. People intuitively:

- See white light around others before their afterlife transitions.
- Feel white light shower them for mind, body, and spirit healing.
- Hear a white light sound (e.g., mesmeric wind, harmonic mantras, blessed rain) transform a pessimistic outlook.
- Know the white light unveils their life purpose.
- Taste a white light flavor (e.g., honey, mint, chocolate) signifying their spiritual gifts.
- Smell a white light scent (e.g., jasmine, frankincense, rosemary) signifying spiritual protection against negative energies.
- Speak a saying for the white light to impart spiritual wisdom.
- Sing a song signaling the white light to release pent-up emotions.

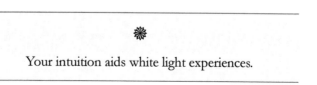

Your intuition aids white light experiences.

DRAWING ON THE WHITE LIGHT

I draw on the white light to cleanse away negative energies from my body's energy field. I intuitively see a rolling inner vision show a luminous white light shower my body—head to feet—for one minute. Afterward, I feel joyful and revitalized.

I also intuitively see a rolling inner vision show me stepping into a bare room brimming with white light. In the room, I receive body, mind, and spirit healing. I intuitively taste white light, like sipping tea, to clear negative thoughts.

119. How do people sense when others will pass away?

People consciously or unconsciously exercise their intuition to sense when others will pass away via several death messages. These death messages differ from those reflecting conclusions, transformations, and rebirths. Family, friends, co-workers, associates, and others spiritually broadcast their afterlife signals announcing, "It's now my time to depart." Their physical deaths occur within seconds or up to years after one or more people sense their afterlife signals.

People have intuitively seen an inner or outer vision show a white light around a person's head or body days before his or her passing. Intuitively felt a persistent urge to call or visit a well or an ill relative; the next instant their relative dies. Intuitively heard an invisible spirit yell a co-worker's name before she's killed due to a violent act. Intuitively known a deadly accident ends a friend's physical life. Intuitively tasted a celebrity's fatal drug overdose. Intuitively smelled a visitor's diseased departure. Intuitively spoken, "His sloppy behavior will deduct him from this world soon." Intuitively sung, "She's bound for heaven this week."

Some people sense that someone will pass away; others also sense when and how. A few individuals ignore or reject receiving afterlife signals; their reaction is understandable. Death messages are graphic, swift, and traumatic. They repeat in similar or dissimilar ways, until the appointed person passes away. One benefit is the chance to visit or call loved ones before they transition to the afterlife.

Ask your intuition to cease communicating death messages when you are overburdened or you prefer to remain uninformed. In the future, avoid saying, "I wish I'd known it was his last day," or "I wish I'd realized her time had come." Death messages restart for the next person's passing because you truly want to know.

Examples: Death Messages

Intuitive Seeing: Honey intuitively dreams an elementary friend dies in a bicycle accident on a rural road. It happens the same weekend.

Intuitive Feeling: Lazarus intuitively feels his aunt's energy fading. Emphysema claims her physical life within a year.

Intuitive Hearing: Crystal intuitively hears her grandfather's coarse voice say, "I'm leaving tonight, dear." He dies due to a fatal stroke, at the same time she intuitively heard his voice.

Intuitive Knowing: Carlton watches TV and intuitively knows a celebrity will succumb after a brief illness during winter.

Intuitive Tasting: Liz talks to her teenage son's English teacher on the phone and intuitively tastes a loss of life. His teacher is killed in a boating accident three weeks later.

Intuitive Smelling: Jefferson intuitively smells emotional pain cling to a graffiti artist. She commits suicide two months later.

Intuitive Speaking: Flo listens to a presenter at a sales conference. She intuitively speaks, "He has two days left." On the third day, the presenter suffers a fatal fall down a flight of stairs.

Intuitive Singing: Pierre intuitively sings, "My hero collects a purple heart." His nephew, a decorated Marine, is killed during combat.

Your intuition alerts you to afterlife transitions.

DEATH DREAMS

Death dreams forewarned me about several loved ones passing away. Graphical images rolled like non-stop action movies. I've awakened with heart palpitations more times than I care to remember.

I intuitively dreamed I attended a reunion in my old high school auditorium. Near the front stage, I spotted a male cousin standing next to a younger alumni. She'd died in a car accident the previous year.

Four months after I had my dream, he suffered a fatal heart attack while volunteering as a local firefighter. He died almost a year to the August day she died on.

One evening after work, I fell asleep on my sofa due to mental fatigue. I intuitively dreamed my sister's high school classmate stood in my former apartment's bathroom. I stared at her radiant, smiling face and intuitively knew she was physically dead. Terrified, I searched for an exit. She kissed my forehead and I woke up.

I phoned my sister who hadn't heard anything from her ex-classmate in more than thirty years. Three weeks after I had my dream, a cousin told me she had died. In my dream, her afterlife signal reigns as her way of saying goodbye to my sister through me. She appreciated their high school friendship.

120. How can I sense when loved ones are around me?

Keep an open mind. Your loved ones physically die, but their souls live forever. Release beliefs that the afterlife is unreal and your loved ones can't communicate with you after they take their final breath on earth. The veil between this life and the afterlife lifts every day. During the momentary lifts, you sense one or multiple loved ones spiritually visiting you and communicating messages of comfort, support, love, and warnings.

Ask your loved ones to show up in ways you feel comfortable with and can easily sense their presence. Selma prefers spiritual visitations while dreaming but not while cooking. Alberto prefers spiritual visitations while meditating but not while driving. Yoko prefers spiritual visitations while walking but not while publicly speaking.

Loved ones show up like you last saw them in person or in their final photographs or videos. Or they choose to show up younger or older than their age at the time of their physical death. However they arrive, you sense who they are during their spiritual visitations.

People intuitively:

- See loved ones in visions and dreams.
- Feel their presence on birthdays, anniversaries, and holidays.
- Hear their recognizable voices "out of the blue."
- Know they visit them at work or home.
- Taste favorite fruit they enjoyed eating.
- Smell strong scents of personal products they used.
- Speak their names or nicknames as they drop in.
- Sing their favorite songs while they stop by.

Your intuition informs you of spiritual visitations.

SPIRITUAL VISITATIONS

As a member of a large family with numerous friends, multiple loved ones spiritually visit me without warning. I intuitively see dreams or visions show their smiling or expressionless faces. They come around to say, "Hello," and then head off. Or I intuitively hear them communicate intuitive messages for others and me.

I intuitively dreamed I noticed my great-great grandmother sitting in an unfamiliar, undecorated room. She died in 1922. No photographs of her exist, but we spiritually knew each other and smiled. The room served as our souls' meeting site.

Driving to my job at 6:45 AM, I intuitively saw paused inner visions show the blank faces of two male cousins. I wasn't thinking about them, but they spiritually visited me. They said nothing and disappeared within seconds.

"Tell her I love her," a family friend stated, as I sat at my work desk and read reports. In my inner ear, I intuitively heard his sweet sentiment. Then I intuitively saw a paused inner vision show his serious face. He'd suffered a fatal heart attack during sleep months earlier. I arrived home; he repeated his sentiment because I'd forgotten about it. I told my surprised sister.

121. How can I improve my intuition?

To improve your intuition, notice how, when, and where your intuitive senses communicate intuitive messages to you each day. Do you receive intuitive messages while driving to your job? Standing in store checkout lines? Reading novels in bed? Exercising in a fitness center? Trust your intuition and validate your intuitive messages. Other ways to improve your intuition include the following actions:

INTUITION BOOKS AND ARTICLES

Study various intuition books available in metaphysical, mainstream, and online bookstores. Or borrow intuition books from relatives and friends. Read magazine and Internet articles about intuition. For the latter, use an Internet search engine and separately type in the words "intuition development," "intuition learning," and "intuition articles." People's intuitive experiences match or differ from your experiences. Use documented intuition techniques or develop your own. Go with what works best for you.

INTUITION DEVELOPMENT CLASSES

Participate in intuition development classes. You improve your spiritual gifts with like-minded, fun people. Search for the classes in local newspapers, in metaphysical bookstores, churches, and newsletters, and on Internet sites.

A wonderful site is www.meetup.com. Type in your city/town or zip code and your interest: intuition, metaphysical, or spirituality. Intuition development classes are taught in classrooms, in homes, via the Internet, and through home study courses.

MESSAGE CIRCLE

Participate in a message circle. It's a secure, supportive environment for people to meet weekly or monthly and enhance their intuition. After a brief meditation, you deliver intuitive messages to other participants; you receive intuitive messages. Instant validations transpire when participants acknowledge your intuitive messages are accurate, as you do for them.

During the message circle, know which intuitive senses communicate details to you. They can switch per participant and per message. Track your intuitive hits and misses to understand how your intuition works best for you. Contact metaphysical bookstores, churches, and newspapers for the locations of message circles in your area.

INTUITIVE SHARING

Share your intuitive experiences with like-minded family and friends. Visit them or contact them by phone, email, or text messaging. You discover how their intuition works akin to and different from your own. Intuitive sharing helps you understand the infinite capabilities of each individual's intuitive senses. Some of the best teachers are those closest to you.

MEDITATION

How regularly you meditate every week is your choice. Five to thirty minutes each time is adequate. Meditate in dissimilar settings, for instance, at home, at a festival, on a balcony, under a tree, in a café, and on an airplane. Notice how your intuitive communication is clearer in certain locations. These locations are your intuitive hotspots.

While meditating, ask your intuition questions for different areas of life. Sense the intuitive answers. Trust the inner guidance you receive, act on it, and validate it.

ENTERTAINMENT INDUSTRY

TV programs and movies, as well as theater movies, depict real people or fictional characters using their intuition whether it's dramatized as a gift or burden. Fictional characters are frequently disguised people too shy or afraid to talk about their intuitive experiences, except through the entertainment industry.

Check local listings. TV programs are subject to change or cancellation. Watch previous and upcoming intuition-related programs and movies on TV or DVD. Previous TV programs include *The Twilight Zone, The Dead Zone, Ghost Whisperer,* and *Medium.* Previous TV movies include *A Deadly Vision*, *Rose Red*, *The Sight*, and *Still Small Voices*. Previous theater movies include *The Sixth Sense*, *Eve's Bayou*, *Gothika*, and *Premonition*.

INTERNET RADIO PROGRAMS

Listen to Internet radio programs in which hosts and guests discuss intuition topics. The programs are streamed or downloadable to your electronic devices: computer, cell phone, and music player. Check listings. Programs are subject to change or cancellation. Internet radio stations include:

- www.achieveradio.com
- www.contacttalkradio.com
- www.hayhouseradio.com
- www.blogtalkradio.com
- www.sedonatalkradio.com

VIDEO AND AUDIO RECORDINGS

Watch video recordings and listen to audio recordings that focus on intuition development. Find them in metaphysical bookstores and on Internet sites. Some recordings are free; others are for sale. Visit an Internet search engine and separately type in the words "intuition video tapes," "intuition audio tapes," and "intuition podcasts." Obtain recordings from the following websites:

- www.youtube.com
- www.thinking-allowed.com
- www.learnoutloud.com
- www.amazon.com
- www.podfeed.net

To view podcasts, it might be necessary to download and install a podcast aggregator on your computer.

❧

Improve your intuition and enrich your life.

Afterword

Your spiritual/human journey continues and more questions about your intuition will come forward. Your intuition automatically communicates intuitive answers for different areas of life. Or use the Intuition By Request (IBR) process to obtain the intuitive answers you seek and expect.

Intuitive knowledge is infinite and intuitive experiences are continuous. Life is your classroom. You are the student and teacher, the chalk and blackboard, and the tests and answers. You graduate with distinction when you trust, use, and improve your intuition. Living the intuitive way, greater joy, love, and success are yours.

BE INTUITIVE AND BLESSED!

About the Author

Darlene Pitts discovered her intuition in 1994 after an angelic encounter during sleep and several prophetic dreams. Re-awakening to the spirit realm, her life changed as she became conscious of and used her spiritual gift in all aspects of life.

She developed her Intuitive Life Review strategy and recognized that she has always had intuition—born with it activated like everyone else. Her spiritual/human journey has overflowed with infinite intuitive knowledge and revelations.

Darlene's life purpose is to teach others how to use their intuition for self-empowerment and successful endeavors. She wrote her first book *Discover Your Intuition* to help people understand how eight intuitive senses communicate intuitive messages. Her second book *Let's Talk Intuition* is written in response to questions people ask about intuition. For more information, visit her websites:

- www.inspirationandintuition.com
- www.zazzle.com/intuitionart

Index

A

Angelic communication, 213
Areas of life, 26
Auras, 202

C

Chakras, 175
Common sense, 51
Conscious mind, 72
Constructive criticism, 98

D

Deja vu, 174

E

Energy boosts, 86
Energy drains, 86
Energy imprint, 211

F

First impression, 71

G

Ghosts and spirits, 205

I

Inner voice, 207
Intuition, 3, 12, 26, 38, 49, 51, 56, 81, 152, 155, 177
Intuition benefits, 27
Intuition by request, 36, 39
Intuition dictionary, 23
Intuition, accuracy, 33, 34
Intuition, adults and children, 181
Intuition, at work, 163
Intuition, beliefs, 60, 62
Intuition, business management, 90
Intuition, changing directions, 77
Intuition, changing others, 148
Intuition, changing outcomes, 140
Intuition, children, 183

Intuition, creativity, 121
Intuition, death messages, 217
Intuition, emotional intelligence, 118
Intuition, emotions, 113
Intuition, exercising, 143
Intuition, finances, 127
Intuition, food guidance, 165
Intuition, health, 167
Intuition, hesitation, 138
Intuition, hidden strengths, 99
Intuition, ignoring, 52
Intuition, improving, 221
Intuition, lie detector, 92
Intuition, life purpose, 129
Intuition, loneliness, 201
Intuition, manipulators, 93
Intuition, motives, 145
Intuition, new guidance, 78
Intuition, predictability, 137
Intuition, reinventing yourself, 120
Intuition, relationships, 101, 103, 104, 106
Intuition, relocating, 161
Intuition, sensing spirits, 220
Intuition, slowing thoughts, 210
Intuition, stress, 114, 115
Intuition, studying, 124
Intuition, time management, 131
Intuition, trusting, 29
Intuition, truth detector, 95, 97
Intuition, women and men, 179
Intuition, word guidance, 162
Intuitive alerts, 171
Intuitive anxiety, 142
Intuitive awareness, 3, 59
Intuitive communication, 11
Intuitive decision-making, 74, 89
Intuitive detection, 157, 159
Intuitive experiences, 13, 14, 15, 35
Intuitive expressions, 10
Intuitive feeling, 6, 65
Intuitive feeling, letting go, 150
Intuitive feeling, pulsing, 68
Intuitive hearing, 6
Intuitive hearing, low sounds, 110
Intuitive hearing, music, 107
Intuitive hearing, phone ringing, 111
Intuitive high, 200
Intuitive illumination, 147
Intuitive investigator, 195
Intuitive journal, 4
Intuitive knowing, 7
Intuitive life review, 44
Intuitive messages, 4, 54, 184, 185
Intuitive messages, acting on, 31
Intuitive messages, literal, 19

Intuitive messages, literal/symbolic, 20
Intuitive messages, sharing, 23
Intuitive messages, symbolic, 19, 24, 25
Intuitive messages, waking up, 80
Intuitive perspective, 123
Intuitive seeing, 5
Intuitive senses, 5, 43, 45, 48
Intuitive signals, 14, 84
Intuitive singing, 9
Intuitive smelling, 8
Intuitive speaking, 8
Intuitive strategies, 10
Intuitive tasting, 7
Intuitive touch, 190
Intuitive trigger, 111
Intuitive truth shocks, 197
Intuitive urge, 82
Intuitive warning, 134, 169

L

Law of attraction, 63
Logic, 3, 49

M

Medical intuitive, 193
Meditation, 16
Meditation technique, 17
Metaphysical rituals, 18
Metaphysical tools, 18
Mood changes, 69

P

Pain transference, 68
Physical body, 9
Physical senses, 3, 48
Precognition, 154
Prior knowledge, 3
Psychometry, 188

R

Retrocognition, 154

S

Scrying, 192
Shielding techniques, 87
Space and time, 46
Spiritual body, 9
Subconscious mind, 73
Symbols, 20, 21
Symbols, cultural, 20
Symbols, personal, 20
Symbols, switching, 23
Symbols, universal, 20

V

Veil, 178

W

White light, 216